Think
Small

Owain Service
& Rory Gallagher

Think
Small

the surprisingly
simple ways
to reach big goals.

Michael O'Mara Books Limited

First published in Great Britain in 2017
by Michael O'Mara Books Limited
9 Lion Yard
Tremadoc Road
London SW4 7NQ

A CIP catalogue record for this book is available from the British Library.

Papers used by Michael O'Mara Books Limited are natural, recyclable products made from wood grown in sustainable forests. The manufacturing processes conform to the environmental regulations of the country of origin.

ISBN: 978-1-78243-632-4 in hardback print format
ISBN: 978-1-78243-764-2 in trade paperback print format
ISBN: 978-1-78243-634-8 in ebook format

1 2 3 4 5 6 7 8 9 10

www.mombooks.com

Designed and typeset by Mark Bracey
Group image on page 168 © Skynesher/iStock

Printed and bound by CPI Group (UK) Ltd, Croydon, CR0 4YY

From Owain

To Sophie and Dylan

From Rory

To Elaine

From Owain and Rory

To our friends and colleagues at the
Behavioural Insights Team

CONTENTS

FOREWORD

Think small to reach big

All of us – from prime ministers, to parents, to public servants – often find ourselves in situations in which we are trying to help someone achieve something. It may be our friends and colleagues, our kids or our clients. Sometimes it's ourselves.

It's a curious and wonderful thing about the human condition that we are often a mystery to ourselves. We really do intend to live more healthily, to not get irritable with those we love and to achieve the goals that we set for ourselves. But the world is full of temptations, distractions and other pressures. Furthermore, our heads and our lives are already full of well-worn pathways and habits. As soon as our minds are distracted, as they inevitably will be, we find ourselves back on a path we had meant to leave, our alternative goal receding into the distance.

The Behavioural Insights Team, or Nudge Unit as many soon called it, was established by the UK government in 2010. Its soft motto was formed by the words in the Coalition Agreement that brought it into being: 'Shunning the bureaucratic levers of the past and finding intelligent ways to encourage, support and enable people to make better choices for themselves.'[1]

Whatever you think of the success or failure of that particular project, and the role of the Behavioural Insights Team within it,[2] it is hard to disagree with the basic idea that, in principle, it's good to 'encourage, support and enable people to make better choices for themselves'. As parents, friends and colleagues, we do it all the time. The question is, could we do it better? In particular, could we use the insights from the last fifty years of behavioural science to arm ourselves, and those around us, with a better set of techniques and skills to follow through on choices made, and achieve the things we want to?

I think the answer is 'yes' – and this is exactly what this book sets out to do. I also think that putting these tools into the hands of everyone is important. I have always felt strongly that the work of the Behavioural Insights Team, and psychology more generally, should be open. This is not just in the interests of institutional transparency, but because this is a body of knowledge that should be 'democratized', or open to all.

Behavioural scaffolding

Building new skills and habits, or achieving our (behavioural) goals in life, involves very much the same art and logic that is required for building a structure. From a simple arch to the Statue of Liberty, building structures requires much planning and careful construction. When it's all complete it's easy to forget the delicate stages and phases it went through to get there.

If any structure is to survive, be it behavioural or physical, it needs strong foundations, and to be wisely placed, to take the weight and stresses it will be subject to. As you start to build, its cement and structure will be weak. To succeed, you will need scaffolding to support its initially delicate joints and links. You will need to keep on building the scaffolding too, protecting your structure from the wind and rain as you go. But do it right, and the time will come when the scaffolding and covers can be dismantled. Your building will stand tall and strong on its own, serving its purpose, whatever that may be.

In this book, Owain and Rory have taken the lessons of the wider psychological literature, and of the Behavioural Insights Team itself, and turned them into the steel poles and joints that you will need to build 'behavioural scaffolding' of your own. Just like steel scaffolding, it takes a certain skill and plan to put it together. Look at scaffolding when you pass it next and admire the techniques used to make it strong enough to support the mightiest of structures. It is braced and connected with a quiet beauty and certainly not randomly scrambled together. This book seeks to give you those same skills, as well as the components you need for your project.

One of things I hope you'll find as you read *Think Small* is not just that you'll succeed in some goal that is important to you – or someone you are trying to help – but also that you will acquire a set of skills that you will subsequently find helpful in many areas of your life. This is certainly what the psychological literature suggests.[3]

It's sometimes remarked that our kids don't come with manuals – neither do we. It's a part of the human condition that our minds and behaviours are complex and multifaceted. Our 'instincts' only take us so far in trying to figure out what drives what we do, how best to shape it, or how our best-made plans can be blown off course by forces and habits within ourselves as much as around us. Hopefully this book will help you to succeed in something that is important to you, or someone close to you.

I also hope it will help the many people in public services and other professions whose job it is to help others achieve their goals. Teachers, doctors, social workers – you are the army of good-natured 'nudgers' whose skills and hard work help the rest of us learn more and live better. If this book, and the research that stands behind it, can help you to do your work even a little better, then it is among the most important things the Behavioural Insights Team has yet done.

Good luck – nudge well and wisely!

David Halpern
Chief Executive, Behavioural Insights Team

INTRODUCTION

The Job Centre

Paul[1] is sitting in a job centre in Essex, on the outskirts of London, waiting for his appointment. Paul is twenty-four, has had a few brushes with the law and has never managed to hold down a job. In the past, that didn't matter. He'd usually found work pretty easily, bouncing between a range of formal and informal jobs. But times have changed. It is May 2011, in the middle of what has become known as the Great Recession, and the employers that would have taken him on in the past are much more cautious now. Paul hasn't had a job for seven months and things are becoming very difficult for him – he's got a young daughter to support and is starting to fall behind on his rent. He's desperate to find a job, so has swallowed his pride and reached out to the job centre for help.

Across the desk from Paul is Melissa. She has spent years helping people to find work, but has become increasingly frustrated by the system. She spends her days assisting jobseekers to fill out endless numbers of forms. Forms to calculate your income; forms to get you onto the benefits system; even forms to confirm you are who you say you are on the other forms. Over the previous year, Melissa had seen hundreds of people's motivation and confidence slowly drain away. She wanted to do more to help, but often felt like she was battling the system, the economy and sometimes even the people she was trying to help.

All that changed for Melissa and Paul when they began taking part in a new initiative. It wasn't your typical multimillion-pound project, supported by a team of brash consultants and lots of new technology. Instead the focus was on the small changes Melissa could make to the way that she helped Paul and others to find work. Though the changes were small, when added together they would reset the way that Paul would think about looking, preparing and ultimately securing a job.

Melissa would normally have begun by asking Paul to start filling in forms. But now she was encouraging Paul to think about why he was at the job centre and why finding a job was important to him. He told her about how he wanted to provide for his family. Melissa wasn't used to having the time or incentive to have these conversations, but found it came very naturally to her. She then asked him to set himself a specific goal for getting back into work. Times were tough, so Melissa encouraged him to be ambitious but also realistic. Paul set himself a goal to find a job in the next three months, ideally in the construction industry.

Paul was then encouraged to break his goal down into steps, like improving his CV, replying to job adverts, asking his friends who were in the trades to speak to their bosses, and getting the new tools he needed for the construction work he was looking for. Focusing on completing each of these steps would help ensure that he didn't feel that the ultimate objective – getting a job – was too distant. They would help him feel as though he was making progress along the way, and this in turn would stoke his motivation.

Then, every fortnight, each time Paul met with Melissa, he

was encouraged to think about what specifically he was going to do and when. He wrote down each of these tasks and linked them to a moment in his daily routine – like making sure he sent out three applications for jobs on Monday morning after breakfast. This would help create a mental link between moments of the day and week and the things he needed to get on with. In addition to this, he signed his name against each of the separate steps. In doing so, he was making an active commitment in front of Melissa to follow through on the tasks they had set him that week that would help him to find a job.

Both Paul and Melissa felt as though they'd been given a fresh start. Melissa was no longer policing people against a set of administrative tasks, and it seemed to Paul that he'd been given back control. It wasn't easy. Paul made application after application without success. But with Melissa's encouragement he stuck with it and, after three months, he found a job on a construction site. Paul later told Melissa that the way she helped him gave him renewed focus in life, improved his relationship with his wife and afforded him the means to support his young daughter.

Behavioural science

The changes we made to the way that job centres help people find work have now been introduced across England and are helping nine million people a year to find employment more quickly. Each of the new practices was based on 'behavioural insights' – ideas from behavioural science research. We will set out many of the most important ideas from this body of research through the course of this book. But before we go any further, there is one underlying theory that is worth dwelling on because it underpins everything that follows. It is that human beings have two different ways of taking decisions and processing information.

This 'dual process theory' was most famously articulated by the Nobel Prize-winning psychologist Daniel Kahneman in his book *Thinking, Fast and Slow*.[2] The 'fast' system operates automatically with no sense of effort or voluntary control. You will be using it when someone asks you 'What's the colour of grass?' or 'What's 1 + 1?' The colour green and the number 2 will pop into your head, whether you want them to or not. The 'slow' system, by contrast, requires your active attention. You use it when someone asks you 'What's 12 × 19?', or if you're walking down the street and you're asked to try to actively maintain a faster walking pace than you are used to.[3] Unless you're a particularly advanced mathematician or very used to varying your walking pace, these activities will feel effortful and will require your active attention.

The fast and slow systems don't just help us decipher colours, tackle maths problems and undertake unusual walking exercises. They are constantly at play when taking any kind of decision – including setting our goals in life, and working out how we should go about pursuing them. The trouble is that most of us are blissfully unaware of the relative strengths and weaknesses of the fast and slow systems, and how they interact with one another. We usually assume that when we set ourselves a goal we will probably pursue it with focus and attention, drawing heavily on our slower, reflective system.

This wouldn't be a problem if we had unlimited processing power. But we don't. We have a limited budget of attention that we can allocate to activities and – as Daniel Kahneman argues –

if you try and go beyond that budget, you will fail.[4] Try working out what 12 multiplied by 19 is at the same time as reading the next paragraph and you'll see what we mean. Or more pertinently, if you want to lose weight, see how difficult it is to maintain a calorie-controlled diet, not just for a day or two, but for weeks and weeks on end. You will find that the cognitive effort required is much more demanding than you might think. In other words, we are human beings. We are not the 'Econs' described in classical economic textbooks who have the mental agility of Albert Einstein and the willpower of Gandhi.[5] We have a finite amount of cognitive 'bandwidth',[6] and this limits our ability to draw on our slower system all of the time.

Many people mistakenly interpret this to mean that the slow system is the 'smart' part of the brain, forever grappling with the 'stupid' fast system, which has a tendency to leap to conclusions without thinking through the consequences. In this characterization, the slow system wants to count calories, but the fast system sees a Mars Bar and snaffles it. But this misrepresents the complex ways in which the fast system operates and how it helps us to live our lives in an ever more complex world. Think about how it felt when you started to learn to drive a car for the first time. It was a struggle and required your constant, active attention. Your slow system was in full mode. Now think about how it feels to drive – effortless and automatic, as your fast system takes over. So while the fast system can trip us up (we eat too much, fail to save for retirement, never get round to finishing that work assignment), it also holds the key to setting us on the path to achieving our goals in life.

This book, then, draws on the latest available behavioural science research to help you channel your attention in a way that will enable you to achieve your goals. It will provide you with a simple framework that will help you to use your slow system wisely in ways that allow your fast system to kick in when it's most needed. A big part of this will involve using your more reflective system today to put in place the behavioural scaffolding around which your future self will act. In doing so, we will be reminding you that the small details matter a lot more than you might expect. To achieve big, you will need to think small.

From nudging others to nudging ourselves

The ideas at the heart of this book are not just based on the last fifty years of academic research. They have been tested over the past six years in programmes we have developed at the Behavioural Insights Team (commonly referred to as the Nudge Unit) set up by David Cameron shortly after arriving in Downing Street in 2010. The Behavioural Insights Team's aim back then was the same as it is now: to take the ideas from behavioural science research and to apply them in the real world in order to help people make better decisions for themselves. In 2010, most people thought it would not work. There was scepticism in the press – most journalists thought it sounded more like a gimmick than a serious new departure for government. And there were challenges from many government officials, who believed that government was primarily about big spending programmes, new laws and bold announcements. Big thinking was the order of the day.

In our previous roles at the Prime Minister's Strategy Unit under Tony Blair and Gordon Brown we, too, were used to thinking big. It might have been a project on what local government should look like in fifteen years' time, if you started with a blank sheet of paper. Or how the entire schools system should be reformed to improve pupils' educational attainment. Big strategic programmes like these are, of course, often helpful. But when they are undertaken, a gap can open up between the strategy developed from behind a desk and what actually happens on the ground. So when setting up the Behavioural Insights Team we seized the opportunity to tear up the policymaking handbook in order to understand better how government programmes affected the decisions people took in their everyday lives. And this required us to start by thinking small, not big.

The first change we made was to how we gathered evidence. We got out from behind our desks and started to look closely at the way that public services worked in practice. We spent weeks in job centres before making the changes that would help Paul and others find jobs. We went on dawn raids with bailiffs, to understand why people were not paying their court fines on time (it turned out that many people didn't even know they had overdue fines). We even waded through hundreds of tax forms to understand why millions of people still fail to pay their tax on time. In each of these areas, we used the decades of behavioural science research to inform how we could do things differently. We also drew on the advice of some of the world's leading behavioural scientists to support our efforts, including Richard Thaler, the co-author of the book *Nudge*, who continues to be one of our closest advisors.

Time and again we saw opportunities for improving the way that things worked – not by introducing a big new strategy, but by making a series of small changes which, when added together, could have a sizeable impact. We showed that adding a single line in letters to late taxpayers (informing people that the vast majority of people pay their tax on time) could bring forward the payment of hundreds of millions of pounds of tax debt. We showed that prompting people with a simple text message, before bailiffs were sent round, trebled the fine payment rate. And we showed how the small tweaks we made to the way those out of work look for jobs could help get thousands of people back into work more quickly.

We knew that these small changes were having an effect because we made a second change to the way the policymaking process worked. We began to test rigorously whether or not the changes we were making actually worked. For every small change we made, we would run a 'randomized controlled trial' in which we compared what happened when someone got the new intervention (a new tax letter, a new job-searching process) with what happened when someone got the equivalent of a placebo pill (the old way of doing things).[7] This enabled us, just like a doctor running a clinical trial, to demonstrate that the effects were the result of the changes we made, not of some other factor.

Testing a policy before you introduce it at scale might sound like common sense. But at the time we started running these trials, it was a radical new departure. It was the steadily growing collection of trial results that started to turn around the remaining sceptics. We were able to show definitively that many of the small changes we were introducing, when added together, were having big impacts. The press began writing articles about encouraging new Behavioural Insights Team findings[8] and government officials began to come to us with new ideas about changes that could be made in their policy areas. The ideas we had used to change the way that policy was being made, many of which seemed radical back in 2010, were now becoming the mainstream.

The changes that the Behavioural Insights Team has made over the past six years have tended to fall into two categories. We have either designed new ways in which governments can nudge citizens directly, for example to save more, get healthier or pay their tax, or we have created new tools to help nudge public sector workers, like those that Melissa used in our job centre programme. In these areas, it's been the Nudge Unit that has been doing the nudging.

This book is focused on a third, less discussed, category of nudge – self-nudges. So whereas classic nudges require someone else to change the environment in which you are taking a decision, in this book we will be providing you with the tools to do the nudging – in your personal and work life. You will most likely be using some self-nudges in your everyday life already – whether it's setting your watch a few minutes early to help you keep to time, getting colleagues to commit to specific tasks at work, hiding away the cookie jar, or using treats to reward your kids for good behaviour. This book aims to help you do this more systematically, however, by providing you with a range of evidence-based techniques that you can use to nudge yourself and those you work with to achieve your goals. This is why, alongside the numerous studies we look at, we will also be telling you stories about how we ourselves have used these insights to nudge ourselves, and to adopt new practices at the Behavioural Insights Team. In essence, we will be opening up the nudge toolbox, so that everyone is able to use these tools in their daily lives.

Thinking small, reaching big

At the heart of this book is a simple framework. The framework is built around seven core concepts. These core concepts and the rules underpinning them are all easy to understand and to apply, but the small details in how they are applied matter and, while a lot of it is 'applied common sense', they are often counterintuitive. For this reason we take time to explain the research upon which the concept is based and how and where you can trip up.

It is also important to state upfront that thinking small is not about small goals. Far from it. We hope this book will help you to achieve things that will really make a difference to your own life and the lives of those around you at work and at home. Our argument is that in order to reach big, you need to start by thinking small. So it's not about reining in your ambitions. It is about adopting a mindset that focuses on getting the small – and often simple – details right, that will set you on the path to achieving big goals.

Think Small is not a checklist. You do not have to religiously apply each of the seven steps set out here to the goal you're working towards. Rather, you should think about this book as providing you with the behavioural scaffolding around which to build your own project, with each of the elements providing you with a different set of tools and support.

The *Think Small* framework starts with how you set and plan your goal, which provides the foundations for your scaffolding. We will then guide you through how to build the supporting poles and joints that will help keep you motivated along the way. This includes tools to help you make binding commitments, set rewards in the right way, draw on the support of others and get helpful feedback. You don't have to use all of these tools for every goal, but the more supports you have in place, the stronger your scaffolding is likely to be. Finally, we will explore how you can create the ties that ultimately bind your scaffolding together, by examining the latest evidence on how to keep going and to stick at your long-term goals. These ties will be especially useful when the going gets tough and the pressures of everyday life inevitably get in the way.

We really hope that by using the *Think Small* framework you'll be able to choose the goals that are right for you and understand the simple and straightforward ways to achieve them, making the world a little better for you and those around you.

1

SET

It is Monday lunchtime and Sarah is sitting at her desk in the office of the luxury hotel she runs. She is surrounded by copies of the new menu for the hotel's restaurant and eating a lobster linguini freshly made by the head chef. Her office has big glass walls, through which she can see the reception. Happy guests are checking in and out, smiling as they ask the concierge to get them a taxi for the airport. Other guests are sauntering down from the on-site restaurant, which has just won an award for the quality of its food, all sourced from local manufacturers and farms.

Suddenly a bell rings and Sarah snaps out of her daydream. She's not in a hotel office any more. She's in the canteen of her Further Education College and in front of her lies not a lobster linguini but a half-eaten plate of tuna pasta. The bell marks the start of afternoon lessons, and for Sarah it's not something she is looking forward to. It's her maths class, her least favourite subject. She's always struggled during maths classes and found it frustrating when others seem to be more capable than her of grasping the concepts. So it wasn't that much of a surprise to her or anyone else when she failed her maths GCSE the previous year and was made to re-sit it. As the bell for lessons rang, she couldn't help but feel it would be easier if she maybe just skipped today's lesson, as she had done many times before.

That day, though, Sarah decided to pick herself up and drag herself to the class. When she got there, she realized that it wasn't going to be a traditional maths lesson. There weren't going to be any equations on the board. She wasn't going to have to do any algebra or work out any percentages. In fact, it wasn't a regular lesson at all. It was the beginning of a set of modules that were aimed at encouraging Sarah and her fellow learners to set themselves stretching goals and then to put in place steps to help them achieve those goals. She was pretty sceptical to begin with. But anything, she thought, was preferable to a maths lesson, so she sat down in front of the computer and decided to take it seriously. The first thing that Sarah was asked to do was to think about the things in her life that she really wanted to achieve and to set herself a 'stretch goal' to challenge herself to get there. She had never been asked to do anything like this before and for a moment her mind wandered back to the scene in the hotel. She was really interested in travel and the tourism industry, and her passion was food. So, when she was asked what goal she wanted to set herself, she decided that passing her hospitality qualification was going to be it. If she didn't get that qualification, she'd never be able to pursue her passion.

Next, she was told that she would need to break down her goal into the steps needed to get there. The more specific, the better. She was given the analogy of a singer who wants to get better at a song. The singer doesn't just proclaim 'I'm going to be brilliant at this song'; she identifies the parts of the song that need most work and then focuses on those parts until she has mastered them. So Sarah started to break down her headline goal into chunks. And this meant focusing on her GCSE maths. That was Sarah's equivalent of the parts of the song that needed most work. Without at least a C in maths, she'd fail overall. So she focused on the things that she could do to get at least a C. She told herself that she needed to spend more time studying and doing mock exams in the library, particularly on algebra and probability. She also needed to change the way she worked, drawing on a few of the techniques she'd learnt through the programme. For example, she found it hard to concentrate for an hour at a time, so she stopped working in hour-long slots. She later explained: 'Half-an-hour slots are really good for me because I take it all in. I have a fifteen-minute break and then I get back into it again.'

The exercises slowly began to change the way Sarah worked. 'It gave me a chance to do what I needed to do,' she said. 'It helped [me to] improve myself and other people too.' And it showed. She was taking home past exam papers to work on them without distractions. She stayed in the library after her lessons had finished. And she was no longing skipping classes. She could more easily see the connection between the individual classes and her longer-term dream of making it in the world of hospitality.

Sarah got a B in her maths exam that year and so was able to start pursuing her next qualification (with a bit less emphasis on algebra). She wasn't the only one. She was in fact part of the biggest trial ever conducted in Further Education Colleges involving some 9,000 learners across nineteen colleges. The exercises were devised by the Behavioural Insights Team in partnership with Professor Angela Duckworth and her team of world-leading psychologists at the University of Pennsylvania. Like all the other programmes that we run, we tested these changes against the standard approach, to see if they might help people to attend college lessons and ultimately to boost achievement. The results are showing remarkable promise. We are finding that the changes are helping lots of learners to stick at their college programmes. They led to an impressive 10 per cent increase in the number of people who turned up to lessons.

At their heart is a focus on the small steps needed to achieve your goals. The learners aren't told to dream big and then assume that everything will follow. Unfortunately, life doesn't work like that. Instead they are told that if you want to achieve your objectives in life, you need to start by being clear about what those objectives are, before thinking about the small steps required to get there.

This chapter is a little different to the others in this book. Before giving you techniques for helping you to achieve your goal, we will first encourage you to ask yourself what the goal, and the steps towards it, should be. But in keeping with the rest of the book, we have put in place three simple rules that will help you along the way. The three rules to goal setting are:

- **Choose the right goals.** You should start by asking yourself what goals you really want to achieve and focus on those that are most likely to improve your wellbeing.
- **Focus on a single goal and set a clear target and deadline.** You should now focus on one objective (rather than your long list of New Year's resolutions), and set yourself a clear target and deadline for achieving it.
- **Break your goal down into manageable steps.** You'll find it much easier to reach your ultimate objective if you identify the small steps along the way to achieving it.

Rule 1: Choose the right goals

Imagine that you are out for a stroll one summer's morning when you're approached by someone who makes an unusual request. She offers you an envelope containing $20. There is a catch, but it turns out to be a pleasant one: by 5 p.m. that day you have to spend the money on a gift for yourself, or to pay off any of your expenses. The woman then continues on her way, leaving you to start thinking about what you're going to buy yourself.

Now imagine exactly the same situation, but with a small twist. You are approached by the very same person, who gives you an envelope containing $20. But this time she asks you to spend it on someone else, or to use it to make a donation to charity.

When researchers Elizabeth Dunn, Lara Aknin and Mike Norton ran this experiment in Vancouver, British Columbia, they found that there was lots of variety in the kinds of things that people bought. When asked to buy something for themselves, they bought earrings, coffee and sushi. When instructed to buy for others, they bought toys for young relatives, gave money to the homeless and purchased food and coffee for friends.

But what Dunn, Aknin and Norton were really interested in was not what kinds of purchases the individuals made, but what effect they had on their levels of happiness. So before the money was handed over, they asked participants a few questions to measure their baseline levels of happiness, and then asked similar questions that evening after they had made their purchases. What they found was that people who spent the money on others ('pro-social spending') were significantly happier than those who spent the money on themselves. They also discovered that the amount of money didn't seem to matter – it made no difference if it was

$5 or $20. The same effect was found when Dunn, Aknin and Norton analysed the levels of happiness of those who'd recently received a bonus of around $5,000. Those who'd spent the money on gifts for themselves or to pay off bills were less happy than those who'd bought something for someone else or made a donation to charity. The more of the bonus they spent on 'pro-social spending', the greater their happiness and this was more important than the size of the bonus.[1] It's for this reason that the Behavioural Insights Team splits in-year bonuses into two pots. One is for the recipient to spend on themselves (ideally on an experience – more on that later); the other is explicitly marked for them to spend on people who have helped them achieve whatever they got the bonus for in the first place.

The reason that experiments of this kind are important is that we are not very good at predicting the things that will make us happier. When it comes to spending money, for example, a clear majority of people say that they would be happier to spend $20 on themselves than others.[2] But as we have seen, when you run an experiment to test this hypothesis, you discover that the reverse is in fact the case. These aren't isolated examples. We dream about a big house in the country, without realizing that the longer commute may make us less happy overall. We buy material goods, thinking they will enhance our lives, when the evidence shows that buying experiences such as holidays and days out will be more likely to improve our wellbeing. And many of us spend countless hours staring at our computer and television screens, when the evidence shows we'd be better off investing in our social connections and relationships.

So, before you set your goals, it is really important that you pause to think about what will make you or others happy. The evidence on happiness and 'subjective wellbeing' is growing fast and is attracting the interest of governments around the world. Indeed, in the UK the government now routinely collects and publishes wellbeing data. Given the broader outlook and nuances of this research, we won't attempt to provide a comprehensive overview here (if you are interested in delving deeper into the evidence on happiness and wellbeing, we would point you to the pioneering work of Ed Diener, Lord Richard Layard, Martin Seligman, Dan Gilbert and David Halpern[3]). But we will draw on a summary of the things that most directly impact on your wellbeing and happiness and that are important to consider when setting goals over which you have some control.

One of the first things you may notice is that money is not on the list. While there is a relationship between income and wellbeing (rich people are generally happier than poorer people), as we saw with the giving experiments, it's not money per se that brings improvements in your wellbeing.[4] It's what your income enables you to do.[5] For many living in poverty, increasing their income (and particularly their savings) is likely to be a common and important goal. But for those of us who are fortunate enough not to live in poverty, we are likely to benefit more by focusing on how to spend our time and money, rather than primarily striving to increase our income. In other words, 'if money doesn't make you happy, you probably aren't spending it right'. So we encourage you to focus your goal setting on five of the factors that have most consistently been shown to improve your wellbeing. The five factors are:[6]

- strengthening your social relationships;
- getting healthy and active;

- learning something new;
- being more curious; and
- giving to others.

Most of us are aware of the importance of our social relationships, but it's only recently been shown just how critical they are to our wellbeing. In a nutshell, people who have lots of social contact are likely to be significantly happier than those who do not. If you see others regularly, are in a long-term relationship, or belong to a meaningful group (like a religious congregation or a sports club), you're likely to experience higher levels of happiness.[7] This helps explain why being unemployed is so detrimental to our wellbeing. It results in a loss of social contact.[8] When you do have a job, social relationships remain critical in explaining differences in levels of wellbeing. For example, if you rate your relationship with your boss one point higher on a ten-point scale, it is statistically equivalent to a 30 per cent pay rise.[9] Strong social connections at work and in our personal lives aren't just good for our mental health, they even affect our physical health – and to a much greater extent than we might expect. One famous review of the evidence, which drew together the results from 148 separate studies covering more than 300,000 people, concluded that people with adequate social support benefit from a 50 per cent increase in the odds of survival over their counterparts with poorer social connections.[10] To put it another way, social isolation has a similar effect to smoking fifteen cigarettes a day. So you may wish to focus your goal on broadening or deepening your social relationships.

Lots of us will have set a goal at some point in our life to become healthier and clearly there are good reasons for doing so. Studies consistently show a strong relationship between health and wellbeing.[11] The better you consider your own health to be, the higher you are likely to rate your levels of life satisfaction.[12] Happier people also tend to be healthier too – the medical literature has shown links between low wellbeing scores and heart disease, strokes and even the length of your life. If you have a more positive outlook in life, you're also less likely to catch a cold, and more likely to recover faster in the event that you do. Healthier and happier employees are also likely to be more productive and engaged at work, which is one of the reasons why workplace health initiatives are becoming increasingly popular.[13] So setting yourself a goal to become healthier, particularly if you consider yourself to be in poor health, is a good idea.

One way in which many of us will think about getting healthier is to become more active. Regular physical activity is associated with higher levels of wellbeing and reduced rates of anxiety. This is why, in the UK, exercise can even be prescribed by a doctor and is considered to be especially useful for people with mild to moderate depression.[14] It seems there are a complex range of factors that explain why this might be the case. They include biophysical responses to exercise (for example by boosting the release of endorphins), but it has also been shown that exercise increases our sense of 'self-efficacy', or our perceived ability to succeed in a task. These benefits can all flow from setting a goal to increase, often by modest amounts, the amount of physical activity we do. So, as you can see, it's important to think about goals that can help make you and others healthier and happier.

A less well known route to improved wellbeing is learning. We usually think of learning something new in quite instrumental terms. You learn something in order to be able to do something better, to pass your exam or to get a promotion at work. But the evidence also shows the impact that learning has on our wellbeing throughout our life. It is well established that learning plays a crucial role in the cognitive and social development of young children, and many parents actively support learning new skills during childhood, but this focus on learning can often tail off as we get older. However, there is growing evidence that learning later in life can improve your self-esteem, life satisfaction and sense of optimism. So it would make sense to choose a goal like learning to play a musical instrument, discovering how to take amazing photos with your new camera, or getting round to signing up for that cookery course. It could equally be a fresh challenge at work that explicitly involves learning something new. At the Behavioural Insights Team we encourage staff to learn new skills, such as how to code or run a randomized controlled trial, but in other workplaces it could include learning a language or improving your presentation skills, or even your whole team learning something new, such as agile project management. Learning a new skill also has the benefit of overlapping with other factors that can enhance your wellbeing – for example, you might learn a new sport that gets you active and also brings you into contact with lots of new people.

One of the most surprising pieces of advice to come out of the wellbeing literature perhaps is the importance of developing your curiosity. At the simplest level, this is about actively seeking to 'take notice' of the sights, sounds and sensations around you and to savour these moments. It is closely related to research around 'mindfulness', or being attentive to and aware of what is taking place here and now.[15] Studies have shown, for example, that if you undertake a two- or three-month training programme in becoming more aware of your sensations, thoughts and feelings, it can positively impact upon your wellbeing, and the effects can last for years.[16] There are lots of ways of developing your curiosity to improve your wellbeing. There is evidence, for example, that having access to green spaces and an expanse of water also helps to improve our state of mind. But one of the best ways of linking curiosity to the goal you set yourself is to think about how you can create 'experiences', which studies consistently show bring greater levels of happiness than equivalent value material goods.[17] This helps to explain why we look back with fondness on the Tough Mudder 'extreme obstacle course' we participated in with our Behavioural Insights Team colleagues, despite it involving being plunged into baths of ice water and electrocuted in the final straight. These individual elements don't sound much fun, but they have the effect of turning a gruelling run into a memorable experience. Better still, along with the physical exercise the experience was also a social event – you have to work as a team to get round the obstacles – combining several different wellbeing elements into one. While you won't necessarily choose to run around muddy fields with your colleagues, you may want to consider what types of experiences you could take part in with your team that can boost wellbeing and staff engagement. A similar logic can be applied to your personal life – both of us increasingly prioritize spending time and money on unique experiences with our friends and families. So when it comes to setting your own goal, you might consider exploring something that will help you to develop your own curiosity, including organizing experiences for yourself along the way.

The final feel-good factor is giving. As we saw with the opening example, experiments have shown that individuals are happier when given the opportunity to spend money on others rather than on themselves. But giving is about more than just money. Giving your time in the form of volunteering is associated with big increases in life satisfaction. Active participation in the life of your local community has also been shown to be strongly associated with happiness.[18] Offering support to others has even been shown to be associated with reduced mortality rates.[19] These factors have led Harvard Professor of Psychology Dan Gilbert to suggest that helping other people is one of the most selfish things you can decide to do.[20] The effects of giving aren't just psychological; it seems that giving time and money can affect us physically too. Biological studies have shown that, when others acknowledge or reciprocate acts of kindness, it triggers the release of oxytocin, otherwise known as the 'love hormone'. Giving, in short, seems to be mentally and physically good for the givers, for the beneficiaries and for society at large.[21]

So you might decide that you want to take on a challenge that involves actively helping out someone in your local community – an elderly neighbour or a community group. You might decide to volunteer your time to undertake a specific project, like regenerating a run-down local area. Or you might decide that you should seek out the support of other people to help you achieve your goal, and to help others achieve theirs – something we will be encouraging you to do in later chapters. This can include your colleagues. Workplace giving schemes have proved a fruitful mechanism for boosting charitable donations and are often very popular among staff, with many corporates now allocating some time for staff to volunteer or collectively support local charities as part of team-building exercises. As we will show later, opportunities to interact with the beneficiaries of your daily work or charitable donations can be a great way to boost staff wellbeing and morale.

So, now you've had time to consider the factors that might help improve your wellbeing, we want to encourage you to use these insights to reflect on the kind of goals that you might want to achieve. One way you might want to do this is to spend a bit of time – perhaps over the next week or two – jotting down a list of things you want to achieve in your personal or work life. Because ultimately, it will need to be you who decides what goals you want to achieve and the reasons for doing so. When you have done this, you should have a long list of objectives. But before you charge ahead to try and achieve all of your life ambitions at once, we need to remember that we have a limited budget of attention, which means we need to focus our efforts on a single goal.

Rule 2: Focus on a single goal and set a clear target and deadline

Imagine that you are an agricultural or factory worker living in India. You've got a couple of young children and you are paid every couple of weeks in cash. You're not the richest person in town, but neither are you in financial dire straits – you don't have to pay off any pawnbroker loans, or cover the expenses of an extended family living elsewhere. But you do want to save more money, so you agree to participate in a programme in which you are given free access to a reputable financial planner who will spend time with you and your family to help you do so. The financial planner explains to you that it is helpful to have a single, specific saving goal in mind if you want to maximize the amount of cash that you are able to set aside. For example, as you have children, this might be to focus on saving to help pay for their education. Over the next six months, your expenditure, income and savings are measured, to see if setting yourself a goal in this way will help to increase your savings.

Now imagine a near-identical scenario. You are given exactly the same advice, but instead of being told to focus on a single goal, you're encouraged to set multiple goals for the various things you will need money for over the coming years. Alongside helping to save for your children's education, for example, you are asked to think about saving to help finance any healthcare needs you might need to deal with, and to set aside money for your retirement too. Which of these scenarios do you think would help you to save the most money? Many people would say that the latter, seemingly more comprehensive, approach of having several goals will help them save more. After all, the more things you need money for, the more motivated you might feel to set some cash aside. In some respects, they would be right. Having several goals helped the participants in this study to save about 50 per cent more cash than they would have done if they had had no goals at all. But these extra sums were small by comparison with those who were encouraged to set a single goal. This group more than doubled the amount they saved.

This research, conducted by a good friend of the Behavioural Insights Team, Dilip Soman, and his colleague Min Zhao, illustrates nicely the kind of counterintuitive point that we will encounter time and again throughout this book. The problem that setting yourself multiple goals causes is that it will ultimately result in you thinking about which of these goals is most important, and by how much, which will result in each of them competing for your limited cognitive 'bandwidth'. Soman and Zhao conclude that the complex trade-offs in the minds of savers (every penny saved for a child's education is a penny that doesn't go towards saving for retirement) ultimately reduces savers' focus on implementing the overarching goal (saving money).[22] And this is one of the reasons why these effects are particularly pronounced when the goals are difficult to achieve. Multiple, challenging goals make these trade-offs even more pronounced, making it even more worthwhile reining in your focus to a single objective.[23]

If a study in an Indian town seems a world away from where you are now, it's worth reflecting on the fact that people across the Western world do the equivalent of setting themselves multiple complex goals all the time. We call them New Year's resolutions. We've all been there. It's New Year's Day, we probably drank too much the night before, so we decide this year everything is going to change. We're going to get fit, drink less, lose some weight, save more and find an amazing new job. And we are going to do all of these things now. The same is often true of organizations, where managers decide that this year the team is going to smash a long list of key performance indicators. But just like in the saving study above, we will very likely find that when we try to achieve several ambitious objectives at the same time, our efforts will be undermined – because the cognitive effort required for us to complete one of these goals will undermine our ability to achieve the others.[24] In other words, for most of us, the problem is not a lack of goals, it's too many of them. So we'd like to encourage you to return to your list of goals that we suggested you jot down in the previous section and to pick one of them.

One way in which you might want to choose your goal is to reflect on the five factors associated with improvements in wellbeing and to give each of your objectives a score out of ten based on the extent to which achieving that goal – whether it's volunteering, running a marathon, getting a new job, spending more time with the kids, improving the performance of your team at work, or losing weight – might improve your wellbeing and that of others. We also want you to be realistic about what you might be capable of achieving. But rather than thinking about your chances of success, we want you to give a score out of ten for how passionate and interested you are in each of these goals. This should help you to ensure that you focus on something that will motivate you to persist and persevere in the longer term, even when the going gets tough. So don't set yourself a goal of learning Ancient Greek when you know that you have no interest in Homer. These two lenses – wellbeing and passion – will hopefully enable you to think about your goals in a different way. If it is not immediately obvious what your single objective should be, it can be a good idea to share your longer list with those who are close to you. Sometimes your partner may be better at choosing your meal for you in a restaurant, because they have a better eye for what you will enjoy eating than you do yourself. The same will often be true for your goals in life, particularly when it comes to the big decisions like changing your job, or starting a big new project.

Now that you've got a single, headline goal, you will need to start being clear about what success looks like. This means setting yourself a clear target. Countless studies have shown, in areas as diverse as weight loss, workplace productivity, quitting smoking, voting in elections and donating blood, that setting yourself a clear target makes it much more likely that you'll achieve your aims than if you just try to 'do your best'.[25, 26, 27] The problem is that this is easier said than done. When most of us go about setting goals, we tend to have laudable aims that lack focus. We make pledges to 'lose weight' or 'learn French', without being clear about what this means in practice. It is likely that some of the things on your list took this form. Does getting fit mean going to the gym more often? But what if you go to the gym, but spend most of your time hanging out in the sauna or coffee shop? The trick is to set a clear target that will enable you to know when you've achieved your goal, and will also allow you to see how you're progressing in relation to it (which, as we will see, is a vital component of feedback). For example, this might be something like 'losing 10 kilograms of weight'; 'running a marathon in under four hours'; 'improving my classes' grade averages by 5 per cent' or 'learning French well enough to read a French newspaper without a dictionary'. There will be very little ambiguity as to whether you have achieved these goals or not. The other important thing about each of these targets, assuming you're not already an accomplished athlete or French speaker, is that they are stretching. As we saw with Sarah at the start of this chapter, setting your target shouldn't just be about saying that you're going to achieve something. It should enable you to focus on something challenging that you want to be better at in the future and which will ultimately improve your wellbeing.

So let's take stock. You've decided what your one goal is. You've set yourself a target. You now need to be clear about the time period over which you are going to achieve your goal. Well-intentioned goals, even those that have clear targets attached to them, can easily break down if we aren't clear with ourselves about when they need to be achieved by, as countless research studies show. One of our favourites is a classic marketing study that shows that setting expiry dates for coupons is better than giving people all the time in the world to use them. Regardless of whether they're valid for long or short periods, the coupons experience what the researchers describe as an 'expiration bump'. In other words, as the deadline approaches, the consumers, eager to ensure they don't miss out, make sure that they use the coupons.[28]

We show exactly the same tendencies when it comes to the goals we set ourselves, which is why it can be useful to set binding deadlines even when it looks as though that might impose costs upon ourselves (more of this in the next rule). This is what happened when students at MIT were given the chance to impose binding deadlines on themselves for the submission of their essays, rather than handing them all in at the end of term.[29] Many chose to do so, despite the fact that failure to hit the deadlines they had imposed upon themselves would mean being docked 1 per cent for every day their essay was late. But the students who chose to impose deadlines upon themselves had a good idea of the effect it would have upon their ability to do their work, and to do it well. They realized the power of creating their own expiration bump. And doing so enabled them to outperform their peers (as did those who had the deadlines imposed upon them by their professors). So what does all this mean for you and your goal? Well, you should of course set yourself a clear deadline for achieving your overall objective. If you're going to get fit, for example, and decide that you want to do so by running a 10k in under an hour, you should say when you're going to do it by.

So, it should be obvious by now that the hard work starts even before getting yourself out of bed in the morning for that first run; or by avoiding smoking that next cigarette. The work begins by thinking about how you're going to set your goal in the first place. Doing so in the right way – by focusing on a single objective, being clear about your target and when you're going to achieve it by – will require a bit of effort upfront. But putting this effort in at the start will pay dividends in the end, by making it more likely you'll be able to stick to the plan.

Rule 3: Break your goal down into manageable steps

It is the final day of the track cycling at the London Olympics. Chris Hoy is lining up in the final of the Keirin, the event in which the cyclists gradually pick up speed behind a motorized pacing bike (known as the Derny). Hoy was looking to become the most decorated British Olympic athlete of all time, having previously won five Olympic gold medals. With two and a half laps remaining, the Derny peeled off the track and the real race began. At first, it is looking good for Hoy, who immediately powers to the front of the pack. But with only half a lap to go he's overtaken by the German cyclist Max Levy and for a brief moment it looks as if the German will box him in. Then, in the final stretch of the race, Hoy recovers and in a fashion that British cycling fans have become familiar with over the years, powers across the line with three-quarters of a bike length to spare.

Chris Hoy was not the only successful British cyclist that year. The cycling team won a remarkable seven out of a possible ten Olympic golds. So when David Brailsford, then British Cycling's performance director, was asked what was behind this success, you might have assumed he would have focused on the dedication of the athletes. You would have forgiven him for dwelling on

Hoy's punishing regime, which included thirty-five hours a week of gruelling training and a lack of willingness to venture as far as the shops in between sessions for fear of undermining his recovery time. Or he could have picked out highlights from the performances of Laura Trott, who that week had become a double Olympic gold medallist. But he didn't. Instead he focused on the approach the team had to maximizing its chances of success.

The approach has been dubbed 'marginal gains', and it has 'think small' principles written all over it. As Brailsford explained on the morning of Hoy's gold medal-winning performance:

> The whole principle came from the idea that if you break down everything you could think of that goes into riding a bike and then improved it by 1 per cent, you will get a significant increase when you put them all together.

By everything, Brailsford meant everything. He used wind tunnels to analyse the aerodynamics of the bikes that were being used and then made them more wind resistant. He introduced changes to team hygiene, like using antibacterial hand gels, to cut down on infections. The team even had the bottom of the inside of the team truck painted white so that any dust that might interfere with the bicycle mechanics could be spotted more easily.[30] By 2016, now without Brailsford, the British team took the marginal gains approach to greater lengths to eke out ever-smaller benefits. They used liquid chalk on the bike's handlebars rather than gloves and even banned bikini waxing to avoid the saddle pain that some of the female athletes were suffering from. The team came home with another remarkable medal haul of six Olympic golds.[31]

We can't all be Olympic athletes. Nor do we have the resources of the British Olympic squad at our disposal. But we can apply this same type of thinking to how we go about achieving our goals, even when they don't include winning Olympic gold medals. It's called 'chunking', or breaking your goal down into its constituent parts. The term chunking was coined originally in relation to memory mechanisms.[32] It is much easier to remember a phone number, for example, if you break down a long series of digits. Try it now for yourself. Try memorizing 0434756863 as a single number, without breaking it into its constituent parts. Give yourself ten seconds and see if you can recall it in its entirety. Now try memorizing a similar sequence, but this time broken into smaller chunks: 0532-799-813. You should find it much easier to organize the information in your mind, and this should aid recall. We see similar effects when we are trying to achieve long-term goals. If we set out to achieve a long list of activities over an extended period of time, we are less likely to achieve them than if we break them down into a series of discrete steps.

There are two different ways of chunking up your goal into discrete steps. The first variant is exemplified and taken to an extreme by Brailsford. The aim is to work out what the different tasks you need to complete are in order to ultimately reach your goal. It was this form of chunking that we used in our work in job centres across the country. Paul and his fellow jobseekers (see Chapter 1) didn't just try to 'find a job'. They were encouraged to break down the goal of finding work into discrete steps – like improving their CVs; making sure they had appropriate clothes for interviews; and ensuring they were making a sufficient number of job applications. You can do the same. If you're training for a marathon, for example, a sensible training programme will be composed of a series of very different elements, each of which helps to strengthen your running abilities in different ways. It will usually involve some form of interval training, in which you vary between running at high intensity and lower speed; doing something other than running – like cross-training, cycling or swimming; and crucially, resting for a day a week, to help your body recover from the training you'll be undertaking.[33] The same principles apply at work. For example, if you're a head teacher and you want to improve your school's performance, you might think about how you hire teachers; the kind of training they receive on the job; what other types of activities support achievement (such as breakfast clubs); and the practices you have in place, such as how you give and receive feedback (the subject of the 'Feedback' chapter).

The second variant of chunking involves breaking down your overall objective into pockets of time or repeated tasks. So instead of thinking about all the different tasks you need to undertake, you might think about how much time you need to set aside every week to achieve your overall objective. One of the seminal studies in this field was led by the renowned psychologist Albert Bandura, who for more than half a century has made major contributions to the fields of psychology and education. Together with his colleague Dale Schunk, he looked at different ways of helping children struggling with maths.[34] The participating children took a maths course in a school setting. They were all given a big booklet, containing 42 pages and some 258 subtraction problems and told that they would have seven thirty-minute sessions to tackle the problems in the booklet. They were then split into different groups. One group was given the recommendation that they might try to tackle six pages in each of the seven sessions they would be undertaking. This was the chunking group – their longer-term goal was broken down for them into easy-to-manage parts. Another had the same overall goal, but were given no suggestions about how to chunk it up. They were told that their aim was to complete all forty-two pages by the end of the seventh session. So what happened? Well, the children advised to break their goal down into chunks progressed much more rapidly. Not only did they outscore the other groups, but they also became more interested in maths – a subject which previously had held little attraction for them. Meeting these daily goals gradually built their confidence and sense of self-efficacy. With their focus on a specific goal for each session, they learnt better and faster than the others.

This second variant of chunking is particularly useful when you need to repeat a set of activities every day, week or month. So if you're trying to quit smoking, for example, it might make sense to start by focusing on a day at a time: you'll find it much easier, and more motivating, than thinking about the next six months without a cigarette. If you want to save money, you might decide to break down your year-end target into monthly sums, and if you want to hit that annual target at work, you should break down your headline objective into monthly, weekly or even daily chunks. This advice is not dissimilar to that given by Professor Bob Boice, who in a study of young academics discovered that the successful ones tended to be those who wrote 'a page a day'. They were much more likely to progress in their careers than the 'binge writers', who periodically pulled all-nighters.[35] A similar approach is evident in agile project management,[36] which is taking root in workplaces across the world – including our office in Singapore – but which is particularly popular among tech start-ups and in the fields of engineering, IT and software development more broadly.

Agile management breaks down projects into a series of weekly 'sprints' and uses daily 'scrums' or stand-ups to agree, prioritize and assign tasks among team members.

The point of the chunking research, whether you break down your goal by time or by the different activities you need to complete, isn't that the longer-term objective is unimportant. Far from it. The conclusion of psychologists is that it's the interaction between your long-term goals ('distal goals') and short-term targets ('proximal goals') that matters.[37] The distal goal helps ensure you maintain your drive towards your ultimate objective (whether it's winning an Olympic gold or improving your performance at work), while the proximal goal generates a clearer focus on the tasks that need to be completed here and now (improving the aerodynamics of a bicycle or practising your presentation skills). In the words of one psychologist, you need to be able to connect your 'distant dreams and the drudgery of daily life'.[38] That's why one of the key lessons in chunking is to ensure that each of the separate chunks ultimately adds up to the longer-term goal.

The three golden rules set out in this chapter should all help to get you on the right foot to achieving your goal. The first rule encourages you to take time to reflect on what things are likely to most improve your and others' wellbeing. One way in which we encouraged you to do this was to write down a list of the many things in life that you might want to change and then to score each out of ten against two criteria: what effect might it have upon your wellbeing? And how much passion and interest do you have in that area? If you're able to do that – and you should spend a bit of time doing so – you will be well on the way to setting yourself a goal that you can pursue with passion and that is likely to improve your life (and potentially the lives of those around you, too). The next steps involved being clear with yourself about what success really looks like, so that it will be obvious to you, and to those who help you, when you have met your goal. Finally, we put a big emphasis on breaking the headline goal down into its constituent parts. These small 'chunks' are fundamental to a *thinking small* approach. They enable you to see the connection between your bigger longer-term objective and the things you'll need to do on a day-to-day basis to get there. So now you've set your goal, in the next chapter we will set out how you can develop a plan to ensure that your daily life and routines support you in making progress towards your goal.

2
PLAN

Take yourself back to the 2008 presidential campaign. America is in the grip of Obamamania. Young campaigners across the country are going out of their way to help Barack Obama in his seemingly unstoppable rise from unlikely candidate to presidential frontrunner. Much was made at the time, and in the aftermath of his victory, about the way in which he was able to connect with voters online. It was even dubbed 'the Facebook election'[1] Yet while it is undoubtedly true that this was the first presidential election truly to embrace the social media revolution, there was another revolution going on behind the scenes that garnered next to no attention, but which campaigners around the world would be wise to pay attention to.

Obama's team had realized that, for years, campaigners had been encouraging people to get out and vote using the same method – by contacting those who'd expressed sympathy with their cause and asking them whether or not they'd be voting this year. Most of the previous research in this field had focused on whether it makes a difference contacting people by phone and, if so, whether it's best to adopt a chattier or more formal style.[2] But given that one of the central premises of the behavioural science literature is that the way in which you frame a question can have a dramatic impact upon how someone responds, the campaign team reasoned that there might be more effective ways of getting people to show up on election day.

Enter Todd Rogers, now at Harvard and collaborating with the Behavioural Insights Team on various education projects, and his colleague David Nickerson, from the University of Notre Dame. Rogers and Nickerson had become fascinated with a set of findings from psychology that showed that if you encourage people to make simple plans, then they're much more likely to follow through on their intentions. The premise is simple. Rather than just asking someone if they're going to vote, you prompt them to think about where, when and how they're going to do so. So they set about running one of the largest voting trials ever run – on almost 300,000 people who took part in the 2008 Democratic Primary election in Pennsylvania – to see just how effective planning prompts could be.

One group of people were the standard group. They got a routine call reminding them of the upcoming election and of their duty to vote.[3] A second group also got a call, but this time they were asked whether they *intended* to vote. The third and final group were asked what time they would vote, where they would be coming from and what they would be doing beforehand. These additional questions – where, when and how – were deliberately designed to encourage plan making. The voters were being asked to make a simple, cognitive link between moments in their day and the action of voting.

So what was the most effective way of getting people to vote? Well, those who received the standard phone call (reminding them of the election) were no more likely to vote than if they'd received no call at all. Those asked if they intended to vote were roughly 2 per cent more likely to vote. But the effect of the planning messages was the most potent. The people receiving these calls were some 4.1 per cent more likely to vote. And most surprising of all was the effect on people living in households with only one eligible voter – here the increase was 9.1 per cent– perhaps because this was the group least likely to have existing plans, particularly ones that relied on others.[4] These results are huge for anyone who thinks and cares about electoral results. As Rogers and Nickerson have pointed out, in the 2012 presidential election increasing voter turnout among eligible voters by 2.1 percentage points for one candidate's supporters would have changed the outcomes in Florida, North Carolina and Ohio. Similarly, in 2008 the state outcome would have changed in Florida, Indiana, North Carolina and Missouri. When an election is relatively tight, in other words, simple plan making has the ability to change the electoral outcome.

We believe that plan making is a key ingredient in helping you to achieve your goals. But, as we will see, the small details of how you set these plans matter greatly. The three golden rules in this chapter will help ensure you get these details right. They are:

- **Keep it simple.** You should create simple, clear rules that reduce the mental effort required to stick to your goal and let you know when you are transgressing from your objective.
- **Create an actionable plan.** You'll find that being able to state how, when and where you're going to take the actions needed to achieve each of these steps will make it more likely that you'll follow through.

- **Turn the plan into habits.** By repeating the same actions in response to the same cues, you'll be able to create habits that make it much easier to achieve your goal.

Rule 1: Keep it simple

A couple of years ago, Owain decided to cut down the amount he drank. He was finding that he was regularly getting back from work and pouring a glass of wine for himself and one for his wife Sophie as he prepared dinner. He'd sometimes wash down dinner with another glass, and if it was close to the end of a bottle, perhaps finish it off while watching a bit of TV. He wasn't a heavy drinker. But there was a danger that he was slipping into a bad habit described in the media as 'middle-class drinking'[5] in which a glass of wine or beer was no longer an occasional treat, but part of the daily routine. In the UK at the time, the advice was that regular consumption of three to four units of alcohol per day for men would not pose significant health risks, but that consistently drinking four or more units a day was not advisable. A bottle of red wine typically has nine to eleven units, so regularly coming back from work and having a couple of glasses risked stepping over these thresholds. Cutting back, Owain reasoned, would improve his health and might even reduce his waistline a bit in the process.

Owain also knew that just setting himself the objective of 'cutting back the amount he drank' wouldn't be good enough. As we have seen, setting yourself vague goals is not the best way of helping yourself to achieve an objective. The obvious thing to do would have been to adhere to the Chief Medical Officer's guidelines of not regularly consuming more than three to four units of alcohol per day. But there are a number of challenges involved in sticking rigidly to these guidelines. The first challenge is a mental arithmetic task. What do three or four units actually look like? What if you have a bottle of beer; how many units have you had then? And it can be even more challenging with wine, since alcohol content varies and most people do not pour precise or standard measures. The second challenge is more psychological. It might seem reasonable to set a limit that can be calculated using a simple equation (it's not that difficult, for example, to divide 750 by 125). But there's a big difference between setting yourself a goal in the cold light of day and then following through once you've already had your first glass of a nice Rioja. This is a problem in any area that requires a degree of self-control, but it's heightened further when you are consuming a substance that has the effect of depleting your cognitive functioning.

So Owain decided that, rather than setting himself a goal which required him to get out a calculator every time he wanted to have a drink, he would set some very simple, transparent rules that make it easy to know whether he has transgressed. Psychologists have dubbed these 'bright lines', and they are effective because they're unambiguous. You know instantly when you've stepped over a bright line, which significantly reduces the cognitive effort required to put the rule into practice. The bright line that he set himself was *no drinking at home during the week.* If he ever opened a bottle of wine on, say, a Monday while at home, he'd immediately know he'd broken the rule. Simple. But this didn't mean total abstinence, which would likely have ended in failure. For example, having a drink with a colleague in the pub after work was OK, as was having a drink at the weekend. Alongside the simple, transparent rule, he set a clear deadline: he would stick to the plan for a month. If that worked, he'd keep to the plan for another eleven months. And the good news is that it did work, very well indeed. What started as a one-month goal two years ago has now turned into a long-running habit. With only one or two exceptions, the no-drinking-at-home-during-the-week rule has continued to this day. Owain estimates that, over this period, it has reduced his alcohol consumption by the equivalent of around eighty bottles of wine.

If bright-line thinking feels like a novel psychological trick, it shouldn't do. As Rory Sutherland, the Vice Chair of Ogilvy & Mather who has pioneered the use of behavioural science in advertising has explained, it is exactly the same set of principles that underlie many age-old cultural and religious practices.[6] Think about the commonly practised doctrine of 'not working on the Sabbath'. Now compare this simple rule with the rather less simple EU Working Time Directive, which limits weekly working hours to forty-eight hours on average over a seventeen-week period, and stipulates a minimum rest period of eleven consecutive hours in every twenty-four. The 'no working on the Sabbath' rule is very simple to understand. It requires next to no work on the part of an individual to work out how to implement it (beyond knowing what day it is). It also has the added benefit of enabling the rest of your religious community to help keep you on the straight and narrow, should you ever be tempted to transgress. The Working Time Directive rules, however, require you – or more likely the organization you work for – to keep tabs on how many hours you have worked over a seventeen-week period, from which you can work out the weekly average. It will never be immediately obvious, if you are close to the limit, which side you are on until you've done the maths.

Similarly, think about the difference between diets that require you to count calories through the week, and those that specify simple rules – such as the 5:2 diet, which Rory (Gallagher) and his wife used in the run-up to their wedding. This encourages you to eat normally for five days of the week, and then to reduce your calorie intake to 500 calories (for women) and 600 calories (for men) for two days. In the words of its advocates, it's 'easy to comply with a regime that only asks you to restrict your calorie intake occasionally. It recalibrates the diet equation.'[7] The evidence seems to support these claims. When researchers randomly assigned dieters to different regimes that varied in the complexity of the rules, they found that 'perceived rule complexity was the strongest factor associated with increased risk of quitting the cognitively demanding weight management programme'.[8] We've adopted similar approaches to work: for example, setting aside Friday mornings for weekly feedback sessions with staff and quick touchdown sessions to celebrate success, or never doing any work on Sundays (this one isn't too hard to stick to!).

Bright lines are one example of the single most important lessons advocated by the Behavioural Insights Team, which we have applied to hundreds of parts of government policy and that should be at the heart of any good 'think small' strategy: make it easy. If you want to get someone to save for retirement, for example, you could provide them with access to a database containing all known pension plans, their historic pension contributions record and the advice of leading financial advisors. If you did all of this, however, lots of people would still fail to save for retirement and, by the time they got round to it, it might be too late. So instead, you could do what the UK government began doing in 2008. You could automatically enrol people onto pension plans and give them the ability to 'opt out' if they want to. You could make it easy. Automatic enrolment is now helping 9 million people in the UK to save billions more between them for their retirement. Making it easy, including by introducing bright lines, is a good example of how you can use your slow, reflective system to make changes that enable your fast thinking system to operate more effectively. As we saw in the Introduction, we are not capable of taking on board all available information, weighing up all the conceivable pros and cons, and then taking the optimal decision on the back of it. But if we acknowledge this fact, we can take decisions that reduce the cognitive burden of future decisions, so that we can focus our attention where it's needed most. It was exactly this kind of thinking that former US president Obama had in mind when he explained why he only wore grey or blue suits when in office. 'I'm trying to pare down decisions', he explained to *Vanity Fair*. 'I don't want to make decisions about what I'm eating or wearing. Because I have too many other decisions to make.'

So we want to encourage you to think about how you might set your own bright lines, and to consider other ways of making it easy for you to do the things you need to do to reach your goal. This is the first step towards setting yourself a plan that will ultimately make it more likely that you will be able to follow through on your good intentions. Some of these will be relatively straightforward. If you're trying to lose weight, for example, alongside simplifying your diet rules you should remove tempting snacks from your home or office (or at the very least, keep them out of sight). The additional effort required to reach them will make it less likely that you ever do. If you are trying to do more exercise, you might think about how you can start to make it easier to do so, for example by integrating exercise into your trip to work (can you get off your bus or train a stop before you usually do and walk briskly?), or by laying out your exercise gear when you go to bed to encourage you to go for an early-morning jog. If your aim is to spend more quality time with your family, but you find it hard to switch off from your work email, you could set yourself a bright line around using your mobile phone – perhaps by never logging onto your email after 8 p.m. or during the weekend. Conversely, you might identify the things that get in the way of achieving your goal and how these can be removed. In the story that opened this book, for example, one of the keys to 'making it easy' for Paul to get back into work was removing some of the frictions in the existing system (like loads of paperwork) that were preventing him from finding work sooner.

Making it easy and setting bright lines for yourself are the first step in the process for creating simple plans. They will also help you to think about how to move to the next step of planning; namely, to start making cognitive links between moments in your day or week and the actions that need to follow.

Rule 2: Create an actionable plan

Influenza is likely to have affected us all at one time or another during our lives. You'll no doubt have experienced the fever and tiredness, the aches and pains and the throbbing headaches at some point. But partly because it seems so common, and partly perhaps because these symptoms start off in a similar way to the common cold, we have a tendency to overlook how serious flu can be. So while most of us will be fortunate enough to make a full recovery after a week or so, some people aren't quite so lucky. Children and the elderly, pregnant women and people with underlying health conditions can easily get a much more severe case of flu, which can develop into serious complications like chest infections and then what looks like a bad cold can turn into a silent killer. In the United States alone, influenza leads to more than 200,000 hospitalizations and more than 8,000 deaths every year.[9]

The good news is that there is a vaccine for the flu virus that has been shown to reduce mortality, morbidity and healthcare costs. The trouble is that many of the people who would benefit most from the vaccination often fail to take it up. Some of these no-shows are likely the result of people carefully considering the pros and cons and deciding that the side effects – a slight temperature, aching muscles and pain where the jab is administered – outweigh the potential benefits. But many more fail to get their jabs because they never get round to making an appointment in the first place or simply fail to show up even when they do make a booking. In situations like these, when you know you should get round to doing something but fail to follow through, a simple plan can work wonders. And this is exactly what Katy Milkman, an amazingly productive professor at the Wharton School at the University of Pennsylvania, set out to test. Milkman and her colleagues teamed up with a big Midwestern utility firm to see if they could prompt more of the company's 3,300 employees most at risk of influenza-related complications to go and get vaccinated. All the eligible employees received a reminder letter about the upcoming times for vaccination clinics. But only some of them were prompted to make a very simple plan. In addition to the dates and times of the clinics, this group was encouraged to fill in the date and time they would go to the clinic. This small change led to a 13 per cent increase in the number of people who showed up. The kind of change that, if it were adopted throughout the US and across the Western world, would help save thousands of lives.[10]

The core principles at the heart of Milkman's plan-making letters were the same as those that we saw in the Obama voting prompts at the beginning of this chapter. They both derive from an idea developed by Peter Gollwitzer, a professor of psychology at New York University, which he calls 'implementation intentions'. Gollwitzer's research focuses on those situations in which individuals seem to have an intention to do something, but then fail to implement the actions required to fulfil their goals. He realized that we are more likely to follow through on our intentions if we are able to make a cognitive connection between our anticipated future situation and the actions needed to fulfil our objective. In Milkman's example, she encouraged people to create a cognitive connection between a specific time and date, and the need to show up to the appointment. It was, in this case, as simple as writing down the time and date by filling in the gaps. The Obama voting example was a stronger version of exactly the same idea. Would-be voters weren't just asked to confirm that they were going to vote on election day. They were encouraged to think about what they would be doing immediately beforehand, and where they would be coming from. This prompted people to think about voting, for example, straight after having breakfast at home. More broadly, 'when', 'how' and 'where' questions play the roles of situational cues, which encourage you to take action by cognitively linking the situation (having your breakfast) with the action (going to vote). As with all *think small* strategies, they don't require you to make huge changes to the way you go about your life, just minor tweaks that will make it more likely you will ultimately meet your goal.

Gollwitzer and a growing range of young academics following in his wake have used implementation intentions in all kinds of areas. In one of our favourites among Gollwitzer's many studies, he mischievously asked his students to write a report of how they spent the afternoon and evening of Christmas Eve. The students were asked to describe how they felt about this time and how much it met their idea of pleasant leisure. They were to complete these reports during the Christmas break, to ensure that their memories remained as vivid as possible. Gollwitzer says that they deliberately chose this assignment because it was 'awkward enough to guarantee a low base rate of completion'. In other words, it was ripe for testing whether students might be willing and able to follow through on their intentions, when faced with the temptations of the holiday season. He then got half of the group of students to form implementation intentions focused on when and where they intended to sit down and start writing. For example, one of the students said that they would do the assignment straight after church on Sunday at their father's desk. Gollwitzer found that those who'd been asked to form implementation intentions were more than twice as likely to complete the task within the specified time period as those who had not made these plans.[11]

If this slightly quirky example sounds far removed from your own goal, you will be pleased to learn that Gollwitzer has recently reviewed results from ninety-four studies that used the technique and found that they can help in relation to just about any kind of goal you might want to set yourself.[12] Making a simple plan that sets out *when, how* and *where* you are going to follow through on your intentions has been shown to be effective at helping people to eat more fruit, increase public transport use, reduce discrimination, get more exercise, diet, improve academic performance, quit smoking and recycle more.[13] This includes the identification of obstacles to achieving these goals through so-called 'if-then' plans. These take the form 'If I encounter situation X, then I will do Y' – for example, if I get home after 8 p.m., I won't log on to my work computer. These if-then plans are ready-made ways of helping you to think of how, when and where you will take the required action.

One of the ways to use implementation intentions to help you achieve your personal goals is to focus on the 'chunks' that make up your goal (introduced in the previous chapter). For a long-term goal, these should ideally be things you need to do on a regular basis, like sitting down to do forty-five minutes of practising your musical instrument or foreign language; or doing sixty minutes of training for your upcoming marathon. This will form the 'how' part of the implementation intention. Once you've got a clear idea of each of the chunks you need to perform, you can start thinking about the situations that might best trigger these actions. The easiest way to do this is to think through your daily routine: the best triggers are things that you will regularly encounter at specific moments and places. This will enable you to be clear about the 'when' and the 'where' of your implementation intention. The trigger for your goal could be your alarm clock waking you up in the morning, or getting back from work in the evening. So, for example, your implementation intention then starts to take the form: 'When I get back from work on Wednesday, I will do sixty minutes of marathon training'; or 'When my alarm clock goes off, I will do forty-five minutes of French reading.' As we will see in the next chapter, and as we saw with the vaccination plans, you can strengthen these plans further by writing them down and actively committing to undertaking them.

An alternative method for forming implementation intentions is especially valuable in helping us to avoid temptations that might otherwise derail our progress – a subject that happens to be the specialism of Gollwitzer's wife, Professor Gabriele Oettingen. The starting premise of Oettingen's work is that we spend too much of our time either indulging in our dreams, or dwelling on the negatives. What we should be doing is a little bit of both. She calls this 'mental contrasting' and it works by thinking about the benefits of realizing your goal and then contrasting these with the obstacles that may stand in the way.[14] For example, you might be trying to diet and imagine the extra confidence that losing some weight would give you when going on your summer holidays, but you also know that every time you go out for a meal, even if you opt for a relatively healthy main course, you'll fall for that delicious-looking slice of chocolate cake with a hot fudge sauce. If you're able to generate these mental contrasts (summer holiday vs desserts), you can then formulate an implementation intention and 'if-then plans' to help you avoid the obstacles that you face along the way. So, having realized that you will succumb to the dessert trolley whenever you go out for a meal, you might decide: *If I'm in a restaurant and the waiter asks if I'd like to see the dessert menu, I will order a single espresso instead.* Or if you recognize that you tend to be more defensive in your emails when challenged and responding late in the day, you could decide: *If I'm writing sensitive emails, I will leave them in my drafts and then review and send them first thing in the morning.* Mental contrasting and implementation intentions, when combined in this way, are especially powerful.[15] At the Behavioural Insights Team, we are using this technique to tackle complex social issues such as childhood obesity, helping offenders back into work and reducing domestic violence reoffending.

Whether or not you make use of all of these techniques, the basic premise remains the same: if you want to achieve your goal, you're much more likely to follow through on the things you need to do to achieve it if you create a simple plan. And the best way of doing this is to create connections between moments in your daily routine and the actions you need to take. This will enable you to go from thinking about doing something (going for a run, eating healthy food) to thinking about when, where and how you are going to do it (when I get home from work, when I'm in the office canteen). If you can do this, you're well on the way to turning your plans into habits.

Rule 3: Turn the plan into habits

In 1971, the American army undertook an extraordinary study. Almost a thousand men returning home from war in Vietnam were interviewed and had urine samples collected. These tests uncovered some very uncomfortable truths. Of the 943 men, 495 tested positive for opiates and, of these men, three-quarters admitted that they had become addicted to narcotics while in

Vietnam. Now, it goes without saying that quitting opiates is difficult – the clinical guidelines for heroin addiction include a sense of compulsion to take the drug; difficulties in controlling drug-taking behaviour; and a physiological withdrawal when the drug use is stopped. So it might come as some surprise that when the group of drug users were contacted again eight to twelve months after their return from Vietnam, only 7 per cent showed signs of dependence, and only about a third of the men had used opiates again. The study was contrary to much of the conventional wisdom: it seemed possible for a large group of people who had previously been dependent on narcotics to quit *en masse*.[16]

So why were the relapse rates for these men so much lower than for other young addicts during the same period? One of the most intriguing explanations is also deceptively simple. The soldiers' drug use was linked to the highly unusual context in which they found themselves. When they were in Vietnam, they experienced an abundance of environmental cues that triggered their drug use. But when back in the US, these cues were largely absent and this meant that these same behaviours were never subsequently triggered. In other words, the returning soldiers never again found themselves in situations that would have resulted in their drug use. And this, rather than their collective willpower, was enough to ensure that almost all of them quit.[17] If this explanation is correct, it could provide clues which might help those trying to break any kind of drug addiction. Indeed, researchers have subsequently found that long-term use of all kinds of substances is much lower among those who experience significant changes in their environment and that relapse rates among drug addicts are especially high when addicts are exposed to situational cues related to past drug consumption. This is one of the reasons why treatment programmes often advise recovering addicts to move to new locations and to avoid places where previous consumption took place.[18] In the 'Share' chapter, we will see that there can also be a powerful social component to these effects too.

We've already seen how important situational cues can be in helping us to create simple plans – by creating 'implementation intentions' that cognitively link our intended actions with moments in our daily routine. But the Vietnam veterans' story holds the key to a new kind of tool that will help us to achieve our goals: it shows how we can break long-held habits, and begin to build new ones. In order to see how this can be done in more everyday contexts than returning from Vietnam, we need to travel to the cinemas of the United States and specifically to American popcorn eaters. Americans eat a lot of popcorn – around 16 billion litres, or enough to fill the Empire State Building eighteen times.[19] For many people, eating popcorn at the cinema constitutes a habit – a regular practice, developed over time, that is hard to give up. To test just how strong a habit eating popcorn in the cinema is, researchers devised a fun experiment in which people entering a cinema were given a bucket of either fresh or stale popcorn. Nobody would claim to like stale popcorn. But the researchers surmised that those who had developed a popcorn-eating habit would be impervious to the taste, whereas those who rarely bought popcorn wouldn't be so quick to reach for the next handful. Just to make sure that the stale stuff did actually taste worse, they got everyone to rate the taste of the popcorn they'd eaten: the fresh popcorn, unsurprisingly, won hands down.

The headline findings of this experiment were completely in

line with the researchers' predictions. People who infrequently ate popcorn at the cinema ate much less of it when it was stale. But those with a strong popcorn-eating habit ate the same percentage of stale as fresh popcorn. It seemed that just going to the cinema prompted those with established habits to eat popcorn, whether they liked the stuff or not. But you might argue that it wasn't the cinema *per se* that was prompting them to eat; it was the popcorn. These people might, in other words, just have a popcorn habit rather than a popcorn-at-the-cinema habit. And to test this principle, the researchers did something clever. They set up a couple of parallel studies. In one, they changed the context of the film-watching experience. They gave people popcorn on the way into a campus meeting room, rather than a cinema, and got them to watch music videos rather than films. When people were in this unusual context, even those with a strong popcorn habit ate less stale popcorn.[20] As David Neal, who led the study, subsequently pointed out: 'When we repeatedly eat a particular food in a particular environment, our brain comes to associate the food with that environment and makes us keep eating as long as those environmental cues are present.'[21]

The popcorn-eating behaviour of American cinemagoers and the narcotic abuse of Vietnam veterans might feel like a world away from one another. But they give us important insights into how habits are operationalized and how they can be broken. If we can understand these two components, we will be well on the way to helping ourselves establish new, positive behaviours that can help us to achieve our own goals, and to break any bad habits that are getting in the way. As with a lot of academic questions, there remains a debate about certain aspects of habit formation, but there is a growing consensus concerning three components, all of which were present in the Vietnam and cinema studies. The first is that habits require a cue or a trigger (going to the cinema). The second is that habits require a 'routine', the act that is performed (buying and eating the popcorn). Third, and most important, the routine needs then to be repeated in a consistent context, and it is this repetition that starts to create an automatic link between the situation that you encounter and the behaviour you perform.[22] This is why habits have the potential to be so powerful: as behaviours are repeated, they no longer require so much active attention or mental energy. Over time, they become automatic responses to the environmental cues that we encounter so that we start conducting the routine in the absence of conscious control, mental effort and deliberation.[23] This is why we'll have all found ourselves occasionally taking the same route to work that we always have done, without realizing that the location of the new office is different.

Contrary to popular belief, there isn't a magic number of repetitions that result in a habit forming. Some say that you need to repeat an action fifty times or for twenty-one days, but very few researchers have actually looked at this question systematically. And those that have done tend to find that there isn't a clear-cut answer to the question. In one of the few studies to have tracked the formation of healthy habits in real-world settings, researchers studied ninety-six students who had just moved to university and were encouraged to repeat behaviours in response to consistent cues (such as 'going for a walk after breakfast'). They found that habits formed in some of the students after eighteen days, but for some it took much longer – up to 254 days. The average was sixty-six days. But what they also found was that, in most cases, the same pattern emerged: initial repetitions caused large increases in automaticity, but with each fresh repetition, the automaticity gains reduced.[24] In other words, habit strength increases steadily, but by a smaller amount each time you repeat the action in response to the same cue in a consistent context, until it reaches a plateau.

So how can we use all this new evidence on habits to help us achieve our goals? Well, there are three techniques you can use – which you choose will in part depend on whether you're trying to break old habits or start new, positive ones. The first is to build on your 'implementation intentions' from the previous section. You should focus on identifying potential cues that you will encounter in your everyday life (alarm going off, leaving the house, arriving at work), and then start to use these cues as the triggers for your new routines. What turns the plan into a habit is the repetition of the new routine over and over until a new habit begins to form. Want to get better at flossing your teeth? Well, keep doing so every time you have finished brushing your teeth before you go to bed. Remember that repetition in a stable context is key – flossing whenever you feel the urge will not result in the same outcome. Want to get round to writing a book? Well, programme in forty-five-minute writing stints after your alarm goes off every morning and before you head into work. It'll feel like a pain at first. But after a while, the cue (alarm goes off) will start to trigger an automatic response in your mind to perform the action (have breakfast, go to study to write).

The second technique is to disrupt the cues that encourage bad habits. We saw this in action with the American servicemen coming back from Vietnam: the cues that were prompting their drug taking were disrupted and resulted in very quick changes in their drug use. And we saw it at play in the popcorn study: by watching music videos in a meeting room, rather than films in a cinema, the cue was disrupted and the behaviour was changed. The key to disrupting the cue is to think about ways of altering your day-to-day environment. For example, if you are trying to lose weight, try getting rid of all the unhealthy food from your fridge and cupboards and replacing it with food that will help reinforce more positive eating behaviours. Or if that sounds like too much of a strain in the first instance, at the very least try moving the unhealthy stuff to the top shelf so that it's out of reach – you will be surprised by the effect that this has in disrupting the automaticity of your response to the cue. There is a strong link here to the 'make it easy' principle we outlined at the start of the chapter. One very effective strategy for disrupting cues is to latch on to natural changes in your life. Studies have shown, for example, that the perfect time to change the mode of transport you use to get to work is when you change jobs or offices. But you can also think about cue disrupters if you are about to go to university, getting married or having a baby for the first time.

The third technique involves keeping the cue stable, but disrupting the routine instead. There are a couple of ways in which you might go about doing this. The first is to do something that results in you becoming much more conscious of the habitualized behaviour, which should reduce your tendency to do it. For example, in an unusual twist to the popcorn experiment, the researchers got some moviegoers to eat popcorn with their non-dominant hand (right-handed people ate with their left hand and vice versa). The effect was dramatic: habitual popcorn eaters ate much less of the stale popcorn.[25] The second tactic is to substitute the old routine for a new one. Electronic cigarettes, for example, are being used increasingly by smokers to substitute a more pernicious habit (smoking tobacco) for one with much less severe health implications (vaping electronic cigarettes). In these instances, note that the cue that triggers the behaviour can remain. It's just your response to the cue that changes. This of course can be especially useful in those situations in which it's going to be tricky to change the cue – for example, if you smoke in response to stressful situations.

Habits are behaviours we perform automatically in response to a cue or trigger, in situations in which that behaviour has been performed 'repeatedly and consistently in the past'.[26] In many ways, habits are the holy grail of behavioural change because they herald the possibility of automatic behaviours – reducing the amount of cognitive effort required to perform them.

This chapter has been about making plans. But not in the sense of spreadsheets and huge to-do lists. Instead we have encouraged you to make a series of small changes, each of which will help make it easier to complete the steps required to reach your goal. One of the most important lessons, perhaps *the* most important lesson in thinking small, is to keep it simple. By setting really clear 'bright lines' you will find it much easier to stick to your plan and will avoid many of the transgressions that can result from rules that are too complicated to follow effectively. We saw that, in order to help you then follow through on each of these separate actions that you need to take, you can use implementation intentions. This involves thinking about how, when and where you will undertake the tasks you'll need to complete, which in turn will enable you to link particular moments cognitively with the things you need to do or avoid ('When I get home from work, I will go for a 5km run'). And finally, we saw that we can take this to a whole new level by turning these one-off actions into habits by repeating them frequently in response to the same situational cues. Forming habits will ultimately make our task far simpler by reducing the amount of cognitive effort required to do the things we want to do – especially if, at first, they seem more like chores than enjoyable activities. Planning out our goals in this way should set us up nicely for the chapters that follow.

3
COMMIT

In the early days of the Behavioural Insights Team, Rory was finding that his commute from the London suburbs combined with long hours at the office and the occasional post-work drink meant that he wasn't getting as much exercise as he was used to. The regular football and rugby training sessions that Rory always had at school and university were on the wane and he started to notice that he was developing a serious beer belly. So Rory did something that a lot of us do at some point in our lives: he joined a gym. This gym had pretty high monthly membership fees, but Rory actually viewed this as a plus point. Just knowing that this monthly expense was burning a hole into his pocket would be enough to keep him using the treadmills and pumping iron. He would always feel the need to get his money's worth. Or at least, that's what he thought.

Several months and hundreds of pounds later, Rory decided to end his subscription. He was barely ever going. And in any case, he felt that he'd worked out what the problem was and how to fix it. Rory reasoned that the issue wasn't his lack of motivation or the gym per se, it was its inconvenient location. So when he discovered that there was in fact a gym in the basement of the Treasury building in which the Behavioural Insights Team was then based, he decided to join up there instead. It wasn't as snazzy as the first gym, but it being so close to his desk would mean that he could arrive early for work, do a quick workout and then head up to the office feeling bright and fresh. He could even pop downstairs during his lunch hour to help work up an appetite and burn a few calories. It seemed like a brilliant, flawless plan. And it was, for at least the first week, when he managed a couple of workouts before work and squeezed in a lunchtime run. But by the second week, he was already finding his attendance waning and thereafter he started to find that he was going even less regularly than he was going to his old gym.

Ironically, the fact that the gym was so close turned out to be more of a hindrance than a help. Because it was right there, he could always tell himself that he'd go tomorrow. It's just that tomorrow never came. Something always seemed to come up. He'd need to finish a report or a briefing for a minister. A Behavioural Insights Team colleague might suggest they talk something over at the pub rather than leaving it till the next day. Rory's wife Elaine might suggest they go for dinner after work. All these things seemed to be either more important or more enjoyable than running on a treadmill surrounded by Lycra-clad Treasury colleagues. Especially when he could always go to the gym tomorrow. Once again, Rory was, in the words of a famous paper on this exact subject, 'paying not to go to the gym'.[1] But thankfully, he happened to know a technique that would help him navigate around them. He was going to commit himself to going to the gym in the future by putting in place a 'commitment device'.

Rory decided that, to get back to his previous levels of

fitness, he would need to go to the gym at least twice a week. Given that he'd failed to go to the gym more than a handful of times for the previous year, this felt stretching but realistic. He then commandeered the Behavioural Insights Team white board, which at the time was located on the wall in the middle of the office, and turned it into our first commitments board. Rory wrote his commitment on the board: 'I will go to the gym twice a week for three months' it read. By writing down his commitment and displaying it publicly, Rory was well aware that he was subjecting himself to a classic behavioural technique which would make it more likely that he'd achieve his goal. He knew that, once a commitment has been made, written down and made public, he would feel a strong sense of duty to remain consistent with his pledge.

He then did something else that he knew would make it even harder to back down. He appointed a commitment referee to help police his efforts and judge whether or not he'd been successful, and set a penalty were he to fail. Owain stepped up to the mark to play the role of commitment referee, which meant that he would judge whether or not Rory had indeed fulfilled his initial pledge, and whether he deserved the penalty he had set himself should he fail. We'll go much deeper into the question of how to penalize or reward yourself in later chapters, but for now it's enough to know that Rory's penalty was a severe one: he would have to don the shirt of the football team he loathed (Arsenal – the nice twist being that this is Owain's team), get it made up with the number and name of their best player (who at the time was Robin van Persie) and wear it to the office for a day. At first, it remained a struggle mustering up the energy to head to the gym twice a week, but the pressure to fulfil his pledge coupled with the potential pain of the Robin van Persie shirt outweighed any of the initial suffering. Then, after a few weeks, Rory found that he had begun slipping into a routine. Suffice to say that Rory achieved his goal and Owain never got to enjoy the moment of seeing Rory in an Arsenal shirt. Perhaps more importantly, since then we have both used commitment devices in our personal and professional lives, from helping us to save money, to setting up overseas Behavioural Insights Team offices, to spending more time with our families.

Making a commitment is relatively simple to do. But it won't surprise you to learn that there are a number of small things that can help to strengthen your commitment, and make it more likely that you'll follow through. The three golden rules are:

- **Make a commitment.** The first step is to make your pledge, and to ensure that this is clearly linked to your headline goal and the small steps you have created to help you achieve it.
- **Write it down and make it public.** You're more likely to stay true to your commitment if you write it down and make it public in some way.
- **Appoint a commitment referee.** A referee will help you stay true to your core objective. The ideal person is someone you trust but who will not be afraid to mete out penalties if you fail.

Rule 1: Make a commitment

Imagine that it's a Wednesday night. You've had a hard day at work, and don't have much food in the fridge. So you decide that you need to unwind: you're going to get a takeaway and watch a film. You order a pizza, turn on the television and are confronted with a choice. On one channel is a film that you know will be entertaining, but lowbrow. Let's imagine it is *Pitch Perfect* or *Batman v Superman* – neither of which will leave you analysing the complex plot line once it's over. On the other channel, however, is an entirely different type of film. Much more highbrow. Let's say it is *12 Years a Slave* or *Lincoln*. Both these films score lower in terms of sheer entertainment, but you've been meaning to watch them for a while, and you think they will be interesting and entertaining in a way that *Pitch Perfect* is unlikely to be. Faced with this choice, after a hard day at work, which do you go for? Highbrow or lowbrow?

If you're anything like behavioural science professors Daniel Read and George Loewenstein and their collaborator Shobana Kalyanaraman, you will have experienced always *intending* to watch a more highbrow film, but then, when push came to shove, typically winding up watching the lowbrow alternative. Highbrow movies, people reason, are those that they have always intended to watch or would have liked to have seen in the past (and probably wouldn't regret having seen, once the film was over), while lowbrow movies are likely to be more immediately 'fun but forgettable'. The researchers explain that, when they first started discussing the highbrow film phenomenon, they observed that many of their friends intended to see *Schindler's List*, but many took weeks before they finally did see it, and many often never got around to it at all.[2]

Like all good behavioural scientists, Read, Loewenstein and Kalyanaraman did not stop at making an insightful observation and then moving on with their lives. They decided to devise an experiment to see how the phenomenon might pan out when people were confronted with different kinds of decisions. So they gathered a group of students, randomly divided them into two different groups and got all of them to choose three different movies to watch on three different nights. But there was an important twist in the two groups. The first group would choose each of the films on the day that it was to be watched. These students would be the equivalent of the person coming home from work, deciding there and then which film to watch. But the second group chose all three movies on the first day. So while the first day was effectively the same for both groups (choosing the movie on the same day that you watch it), days two and three were different – the second group were making choices about what to watch in the future, whereas the first were always grounded in the present. The question was whether, by encouraging the students to commit to future choices, the decisions that they took would better reflect what they intended to do (*Schindler's List*) rather than what they chose to do on the spur of the moment (*Batman v Superman*). And that is exactly what happened. In the first group, the one that got to choose a film every day, most of the students chose a lowbrow film each time. But in the second group, a lowbrow film was only chosen most frequently on the first day. For subsequent days, when the students were thinking more about what they intended to do, they were more likely to choose a highbrow film.[3]

This simple experiment might seem like a frivolous foray into the world of cinematography. But it also teaches us something profound concerning how we think about the future. We tend to prefer immediate 'vices' (lowbrow films, burger and chips, surfing the internet at work) to immediate 'virtues' (highbrow films, grilled chicken and salad, getting that final report written), 'since the vice offers a larger reward in the present'.[4] Behavioural scientists call it 'present bias' – we prefer rewards today over bigger gains tomorrow, and delay effortful decisions and actions, even when we know we probably shouldn't. We prefer cake and relaxation today, and brown rice and exercise tomorrow. We spend money in our pocket today over saving for retirement. We fail to tackle global problems like climate change because the costs are borne upfront but the benefits of acting are felt long into the future. It's almost as if we have a present self, who tends to like ice cream and beer, and a future self who has a different, more virtuous set of preferences, such as abstaining from dessert and drinking sparkling water. The problem, of course, is that at some point our future selves will in fact be our present selves. And this is the clever part of Read, Loewenstein and Kalyanaraman's study. They were able to show that by getting our present selves to think about our future self, and bind them into a decision in advance, it is possible to overcome this temporal hurdle. That, in essence, is what a commitment device is. It's a pledge made by your present self that binds your future self to a more virtuous path, in the knowledge that in the future it will be your present self taking the decisions.[5]

So if you know that you are going to find it hard, like Rory, to get to the gym regularly, or if you know that it's going to be tough to keep up the language lessons because your future self might prefer going to the pub instead of conjugating verbs, you should think about setting yourself a commitment. In the next sections, we'll learn about how to strengthen these commitments. But for now it's enough to know that making a commitment – to go the gym, to attend your language lessons – is the important, first step. When you do this, you can either commit to your ultimate objective (running a marathon in under four hours), or you can link it with the most troublesome steps that you have identified to achieving that objective (going for a run three times per week). And you should link this commitment to the rewards or penalties you set yourself (how to set these incentives is the subject of the 'Reward' chapter). That is the best way of making your commitment binding, with definite consequences if you fail to follow through. If you do all of these things, you will likely find that you have a strong desire to remain consistent with the promises that you have made, and you will feel uncomfortable about breaking the commitment you make. This anticipated discomfort will help you stay on course.[6]

One of our favourite examples of a commitment device being used to help people achieve a stretching goal relates to savings and employs all of these mechanisms. Some 700 individuals were given the option of opening either a straight savings account or a commitment savings account, which required clients to pledge not to withdraw funds until they reached a specific goal they had set themselves. The savers could either decide to set a goal linked to when large sums of money were needed (such as Christmas or for school), or they could set one linked to a set amount of money. They had complete flexibility over what that goal might be, but once the goal was set, it was explained that the commitment would be binding. In other words, they would only receive the money if they met their target or once they reached their target date.[7] After twelve months, the researchers measured the average bank account savings of those who had been offered the commitment accounts relative to a control group of people who had not, and they found that average savings balances increased by 81 per cent for those who'd been offered the accounts.

One of the reasons that we like this study is that no one was forced to take up the accounts. In fact, there were good grounds for thinking that no one would: they offered no financial incentives and prevented people from accessing money at short notice. And yet between a quarter and a third of everyone given the opportunity to open a commitment savings account decided to take up the offer. That so many people were prepared to take up the accounts was an important finding in its own right, demonstrating that a decent proportion of savers were sufficiently aware of their cognitive frailties to bind their future choices.[8] And in fact when we stop to think about it, we routinely use commitment devices all the time. Disgruntled parents ask their children not just to tidy their rooms, but to promise to do so. We schedule workouts with a partner in part because we know that failing to follow through will disappoint the other person, or we enter half-marathons six months in the future as we know that this will force us to train. Similarly, we ask our colleagues what they will do before the next meeting, to increase the likelihood they will follow through. There is even evidence showing that people are starting to buy their food online in part because it helps them to commit to purchases that are in line with their future self's preferences, and thus to avoid making the impulse buys that their present self craves.[9]

So it appears that, in all kinds of fields, we seem to understand intuitively that we will face temptations in the future that our current selves would rather our future selves avoided. We also seem to understand that a good way of avoiding these paths is to commit to future action. So, once you have set your goal and worked out the steps you need to achieve it, you should commit to achieving that goal and/or the separate steps to get there.

Rule 2: Make your commitment public and write it down

One of the most famous experiments in social psychology was a test of 'conformity' – in other words, of how susceptible we are to social pressure from a group. In the classic experiment, conducted by Solomon Asch in the 1950s, participants were shown two cards. One had a line on it, the other three lines. The challenge was to say which of the three lines matched the single line on the other card. It was a deceptively simple task, such that in normal circumstances, individuals matching the lines would make a mistake less than 1 per cent of the time (and to be honest, you have to question what the 1 per cent were doing when asked the question). You can try it for yourself below – which of the lines in the row of three matches the line by itself?

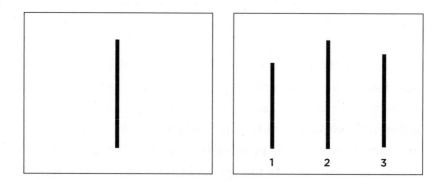

But this being a psychology experiment, the real test was not whether it was possible to match the lines. It was what happened if you got someone to contradict your judgement about which lines matched. In Asch's experiments, an individual is put in a room with a group of actors who are instructed to get the answers deliberately and consistently wrong. The test is whether the individual participant is willing to give a clearly erroneous answer as a result of the social pressure exerted by the group. If this is the first time you have come across such experiments, you may be surprised by the core finding – which is that the individual accepted the misleading majority's wrong judgements 37 per cent of the time. In the 1950s, in the aftermath of the Holocaust and the beginning of the Cold War, this was a worrying finding: it seemed we were much more likely to succumb to group pressure than we might like to think. 'That we have found the tendency to conformity in our society so strong that reasonably intelligent and well-meaning young people are willing to call white black is a matter of concern', wrote Solomon Asch.[10] But while these headline findings were indeed surprising and potentially worrying for social psychologists at the time, it was also recognized that small changes in the way that an individual's view was put forward would have a considerable effect on their willingness to stick to their guns.

Following in the lead of Solomon Asch, Morton Deutsch and Harold Gerard ran the experiments again, but with a series of subtle variations that were designed to examine whether different kinds of commitments might strengthen the resolve of the participants.[11] Some people participated in the same way that individuals had done in the original experiments. They saw the lines, made a judgement in their heads and were then subjected to the views of others. But others had a slightly different set-up. Rather than just keeping it in their heads, they were told to write down their judgements before telling others what it was. The question was whether writing it down might strengthen the individual's commitment to the answer they had arrived at and would prevent them being so easily swayed by group pressure.[12] The experiment results, when no one wrote down their answers, were very similar to the original Asch experiments. Individuals felt the same pressure to conform and continued to make a series of erroneous judgements about the lengths of the lines they'd seen. But when the judgements were written down in advance on a piece of paper, the errors were hugely reduced – by more than three-quarters.[13]

This niche set of experiments, conducted sixty years ago, might feel a world away from the goals you set yourself. But they reveal a set of common truths about human behaviour that we can use to strengthen the commitments we make. The first, simple step, is to do exactly what the individuals in the re-running of the experiment did: write your commitment down. You can write it on a board in a public space, as Rory did with his gym commitment. Or you can write it on a piece of paper in front of your commitment referee (we'll meet these characters in the next section). Writing down a commitment, and even going as far as signing your name against the pledges you make, is a surprisingly effective way of encouraging consistency in behaviour – one of the reasons that the technique is employed so frequently in modern life. We sign contracts committing us to employment, getting married and buying houses. These are only considered to be binding – to commit us to future action – once we've written, dated and signed our name. Organizations around the world ask their employees to set themselves objectives for what they will achieve through the year, which are written down and agreed with their managers. Even shopping lists seem to be effective ways of changing the way we shop. It's not just that they help us to remember what to buy, they also help us to avoid impulse buys in a similar way that online shopping does: by pre-committing us to future action.[14] So once you have made a commitment, write it down.

If writing the commitment down helps to raise the stakes of a commitment, then making it public can turbocharge it. In other words, you shouldn't keep your written commitment to yourself. Indeed, one of the things that made the written commitments powerful in the Deutsch and Gerard studies was the very real possibility that these prior commitments would be revealed publicly. To understand the mechanisms at play in a public commitment, we like to go back to a fun study using a scenario that will be familiar to us all, conducted by the psychology professor Thomas Moriarty.[15] It was first brought to our attention by Robert Cialdini, whose classic book *Influence* has informed the work of the Behavioural Insights Team over the years.[16]

The scene is a summer day at Jones Beach in New York. Imagine that you're there now and think about how you might respond to the following scenario. Out of the corner of your eye, someone comes and places a blanket on the beach within five feet of you and turns on a portable radio to a local radio station at a fairly high volume. After a couple of minutes, the person asks if you have a light for the cigarette they are about to smoke and then walks away, out of sight. A few minutes later, a shady-looking man appears. The man walks up to the blanket, picks up the radio (still playing loudly) and quickly walks away with it. What do you do? If you're anything like most people in the study, you do nothing. You allow the thief to take the radio and do not intervene. Why would you, you might ask yourself – you could be risking personal harm, and you're not sure who the radio owner is anyway. But now imagine exactly the same scenario, but with one subtle twist. Rather than asking you for a light, the antisocial radio enthusiast approaches you before they head up the beach and says, 'Excuse me, I'm going up to the boardwalk for a few minutes…would you watch my things?' In other words, they elicit from you a direct, public commitment. What do you do in this scenario when the thief appears to take the radio? If you're like the beachgoers of New York, after publicly committing to watching the things of a total stranger you will become a completely different person. When the experiment was run, 95 per cent of people intervened – only one in twenty failed to challenge the thief.

Much like writing down a commitment in advance, making it public creates a stronger incentive to be consistent than if we had simply made the pledge in our heads. Whereas the process of writing down a commitment internalizes the social pressure in which we hold expectations about own behaviour, making it public exposes this internal pressure to others. It's the consistency of our behaviour in the eyes of others that is important.[17] You've said that you will look after someone's things; now how will you feel when asked what you did by the person who you made the commitment to? The need to maintain public consistency is one of the reasons why hung juries are more likely to occur when jurors are made to express their initial opinions through a visible show of hands rather than by secret ballot. Once jurors state their initial views publicly, they become reluctant to change these views publicly.[18] If we stop to think about it, we will realize that we already make use of public commitments – often for those things that are considered to be the most important of all the decisions we're likely to make. There's a reason, for example, why we invite people to our weddings to hear us say our vows, rather than just agreeing to be married to our spouse. There is even some evidence that shows an inverse relationship between the number of people you have at your wedding and your subsequent chances of getting divorced. Couples who elope are more than twelve times more likely to end up divorced than couples who get married at a wedding ceremony with more than 200 people.[19] There are, of course, many confounding factors at play here – it may well be that couples who get married on their own are more likely to be doing so impulsively. Nevertheless, this is strongly consistent with other work suggesting that making your commitment public in front of a group of family and friends may provide you with the motivation and networks needed to make you more likely to stick together 'for better or worse'.[20] So think about ways you can make your commitments public – for example, you may commit to your team to send weekly updates on key decisions, or commit publicly on your organization's website to publish annual reports.

As with many other aspects of a *think small* approach, however, the way you make your commitment public is important. Think back to how Rory made his commitment to get fit. He didn't just announce his goal to his colleagues and be done with it. There is some evidence that *just* announcing your intentions to reach a goal in this way can backfire, and doesn't create the requisite bind of consistency. It seems that we get a small buzz from telling people about our goals, regardless of whether we actually then follow through on our intentions – especially where these are likely to carry some social kudos (such as writing a novel or recycling more).[21] But something different happens when we go a step further. So that's why Rory didn't just announce his good intentions. He set out publicly the steps that he was going to take to achieve his goal, by writing the latter down on the office whiteboard. This is the hallmark of a good commitment device. It's also why it's important, in applying a *think small* approach, to link your commitment to the plan-making and goal-setting activities that were the focus of the previous chapters. It makes a big difference to commit to undertaking the specific steps you need to make to achieve your goal, rather than simply declaring your intention to achieve something. As ever, the small details matter.

Rule 3: Appoint a commitment referee

There is a great scene in the American comedy series *Curb Your Enthusiasm* in which Larry David is asked by a friend to help her to avoid eating dessert by playing the role of her 'dessert referee'.[22] He is asked not to let her eat any of the fabulous desserts that she has prepared 'no matter what'. However, later that evening, she heads to the dessert table and picks up a large piece of cake, which Larry spots and prevents her from eating, taking the cake out of her hands.

> Friend: 'I'm just going to have a bite.'
> Larry: 'No, no, no. You told me specifically not to let you have any dessert.'
> Friend: 'I appreciate it Larry, but I changed my mind.'
> Larry: 'Yes, but you said "no matter what".'
> Friend: 'But you know what, now I'm changing it. And I'm saying thank you for helping me but I'm going to have some cake.'

Larry: 'But you can't change it, that's why you say "no matter what". This is the "what". That's why you asked me and not those other people, because you knew I wouldn't let you.'

Group: 'Come on, Larry, let her have it.'

Larry: 'But she said no matter what.'

Anyone who's ever watched *Curb Your Enthusiasm* will not be too surprised to learn that, following Larry David's intervention, the scene descends into chaos. But though his execution may have left a lot to be desired, he had stumbled across a number of principles that the latest behavioural science research is showing can be of great importance in helping you stick to your goals. The first was Larry's friend's recognition, at the heart of all good commitment devices, that her future self would face temptations that would be challenging to resist. The second was the understanding that you are more likely to be able to follow through on your commitment if you appoint someone to act as your commitment referee: someone who will monitor your compliance and determine whether you have succeeded in meeting your goal.

Two of the behavioural scientists who've thought most about the importance of commitment referees are Dean Karlan and Ian Ayres. They also helped to set up the website stickK. com, specifically to help people make and follow through on their commitments. StickK.com encourages people to create a commitment contract – a binding contract you sign to help you follow through on your intentions. This is very much in line with the principles we have already seen – writing it down and making it public. Over the years Karlan and Ayres have gathered lots of data on which commitment contracts are most likely to be met and have found that one of the most effective ways of achieving your goal is to appoint a commitment referee. People who have a referee are about 70 per cent more likely to report success in achieving their goals than those who do not.[23] But as Karlan and Ayres have realized, and Larry discovered to his peril, the appointment of a referee can be fraught with complications. When Ayres came to present some of his latest findings to the Behavioural Insights Team, he gave two important pieces of advice. The first is that you have to trust that your referee will be fair. It's no good appointing someone who will revel in your ill fortune, or conspire against you. A poor choice of dessert referee, for example, would be someone who enjoys waving tiramisu in your face in order to see you fail. The second, even more important consideration is that you have to believe that your referee will be prepared to enforce the commitment by following through on any penalties (or rewards) that you have set (the subject of the next chapter).

Many people might think that someone very close to them (such as a romantic partner) might be best placed to be their commitment referee. But while the evidence suggests that it is effective to make your pledge in front of a romantic partner (i.e. the make-it-public part),[24] these same people can often make poor referees precisely because they are more understanding of any noncompliant behaviour ('You've had a hard day!'). In other words, they may be more likely to conspire with you in unhelpful ways ('Why do you have to go to the gym tonight when we could be going out?') and are therefore more likely to be unwilling to enforce the terms of your commitment contract. So Ayres' advice is not to designate 'either an enemy or a soft-hearted friend to be your referee'. For this purpose, a trusted colleague might be less likely to conspire with you than your boyfriend or girlfriend. When Rory set about committing to his new exercise regime, for example, he knew that Owain was much more likely to enforce his penalty than his wife, who might be more understanding if he failed to visit the gym often enough – particularly if it was because, for example, they both had plans to visit the cinema or go for dinner that evening. In hindsight, the only mistake that Rory and Owain made in setting the terms of the commitment was that the punishment represented a conflict of interest for Owain: it would have given him a significant amount of joy to see Rory having to wear an Arsenal shirt. Thankfully for Rory, this never came to be.

The use of commitment referees has huge potential in all kinds of areas. We saw in the example that opened this book how commitment devices don't just help you to meet your personal goals, but can also be useful for helping you to encourage others to achieve theirs at work too. The programme we put in place in job centres helped to get people back to work faster. At the heart of that new programme was a focus on setting stretching goals, breaking them down and then *committing* to each of the separate activities. Paul committed to working on his CV, making applications for jobs and buying new tools to help prepare him for the jobs he was applying for. He specified when he was going to do these things (part of his plan-making activities). And he did all of this in the presence of Melissa, his job advisor, who acted as Paul's commitment referee. There is a world of difference between Melissa asking Paul whether he has undertaken a set of administrative tasks that are requirements for approving his benefit claims and acting as someone's referee in relation to the goals that *they themselves* have committed to. When Paul signed his commitment contract with a pledge to 'sign up to five job sites' that week and to bring an updated CV and cover letter in for his next meeting with Melissa, it was him who was making the commitments. He'd be letting himself down if he failed to follow through, but equally Melissa would have a concrete pledge of Paul's with which to hold him to account. Notice, however, that Melissa's role was not to find out where Paul had gone wrong. She was not doing the equivalent of waving tiramisu in the face of someone who was trying to avoid eating cake. Rather, she was there to help and support Paul, but she was also able to step back and judge whether or not Paul had achieved his goals.

Up to now, we've assumed that your commitment referee will help you to monitor your progress and be present when you're setting your goal in the first place. But we think that over the coming years, a range of new technologies may well start providing us with this service in ways that cut down on any of the administrative effort required. The rise of smart phones, wearable devices and apps enable us to track physical activity, spending, sleep and our weight. It might be that, over time, these new devices can be combined with the insights that show the benefit of having a trusted, nominated individual to help you follow through. There are already some emerging examples of this kind of interaction in practice – examples that combine smart technology with a nominated commitment referee. One such example is GlowCaps,[25] which are designed to help people adhere to their medication. GlowCaps are wireless-enabled caps for standard prescription bottles that light up and play a ring tone to remind you to take your medication. The device records information concerning each time the medicine bottle is opened, and reminder calls are sent to the patient if the bottle isn't opened within one to two hours of the designated time. In addition, patients are encouraged to nominate a commitment referee (for example a family member, friend, caregiver or doctor) who will also receive an emailed medication adherence summary each week. The hope is that the nominated referee will act as a form of external support to help boost medical adherence.

Commitment referees, then, can come in a number of different forms, but several principles seem to be important in ensuring that your referee will help you achieve your goals. In particular, we've seen how important it is to get the right kind of referee – someone who is fair but also willing to administer the penalties or rewards you set yourself. We've also seen how the previous steps, in particular writing down your commitment, help to ensure that everyone is clear about what the goal is, so that it can more easily be enforced. All of these small steps, we hope, should make it easier for you to stay motivated, and easier for your commitment referee to keep you on the straight and narrow.

Commitment devices are useful because our present selves seem to have different preferences from our future selves. If we weren't aware of this conflict, it would be hard to commit to anything. But thankfully, it seems that human beings know full well their own frailties, which is why many of us seem prepared to lock ourselves into choices that bind future action, like opening savings accounts that keep our money locked up until we reach our savings goals. So commitment devices work, first and foremost, because we are prepared to enter into them due to an existing awareness of our self-control issues. But once we have made them, they work for a different reason; when we have made a commitment, we encounter pressures to behave consistently with the pledge that we have made and knowing this enables us to strengthen the commitments we make. By writing down our commitments and making them public, we not only increase the internal pressure upon ourselves to behave consistently with our commitment, but also feel interpersonal pressure to do the same. And this can be further enhanced by appointing yourself a commitment referee. Not someone who is there to trip you up or help find excuses, but someone who can provide the support you need to keep you on track. That commitment referee will also be the person who is best placed to decide whether or not you are deserving of the reward you set yourself. How you do this is the subject of the next chapter.

become a bit more complicated as your children grow up. You may have wondered what types of rewards would be appropriate, for example, to encourage your teenage children to study hard at school in the run-up to important exams. You may even have wondered whether it's appropriate to reward (or bribe!) your children at all for things you feel they should be doing anyway.

Parents aren't the only ones pondering these types of questions. Many teachers, head teachers, academics and policy makers have wrestled with how best to encourage kids to improve their grades. That's why the work of people like Simon Burgess, a Professor of Economics at the University of Bristol, is so important. Burgess and his team of researchers have been running numerous studies in schools across England.[1] One of the largest looks at whether providing pupils with rewards can help to increase effort and engagement and ultimately the grades they achieve. Covering sixty-three schools and some 10,000 pupils in the final year of their GCSE exams, Burgess's team divided the schools into three distinct groups. The first group acted as the control – none of their pupils would get any rewards. The second group of schools were given financial rewards. These rewards were based on their attendance, behaviour, classwork and homework over four separate periods of five weeks. The incentives were pretty big for fifteen and sixteen year olds: you could get up to £80 for each of the five week periods, or £320 overall. The third group got a different kind of reward. These pupils were instead offered the chance to attend events that were chosen by student representatives. They could win tickets during each of the five week periods that would enable them to go to up to two events during the year – making them much less costly overall than the cash rewards. The events included trips to Wembley (home of the England football team), the Houses of Parliament and theme parks.

Before we reveal the results, try putting yourself in the shoes of the teachers and parents of these sixteen year olds. Have a think about whether you would be inclined to support a school that set up an incentive programme of this kind, or whether you'd be inclined to use one at home to motivate your child. What happened in practice demonstrated the importance of the small details of the incentives programme. It turned out that their impact depended on the circumstances of the pupils. The rewards had next to no impact on those pupils who were already expected to do well. It seemed that these pupils didn't need an extra incentive. They were already motivated to perform. But for around half of the pupils, the effects of both the financial and the non-financial rewards were substantial (with slightly bigger effects for the more costly cash rewards). The effects were especially big for those from lower income groups. For maths and science GCSEs, the incentives eliminated about half of the difference you would have expected to see between pupils eligible for free school meals and the other pupils, and was particularly effective at improving the grades of those expected to do less well.

This study might feel like an interesting diversion into the minds of teachers, parents and teenagers in the run-up to an important set of exams. But the results provide us with important lessons into some of the very real challenges in using rewards to motivate behaviour. Top of this list is the concern that financial rewards can 'crowd out' intrinsic motivation. Lots of studies, some of which we will examine in this chapter, have documented how paying people to do things that they are already motivated to do can backfire. As we will see, and as Burgess's study neatly shows, it's not that financial incentives in general don't work. Far from it. It's that financial incentives need to be properly targeted, so that they provide a sufficiently meaningful incentive to the individual receiving them in the context in which they are given. An £80 reward to a pupil who doesn't respond to an incentive to work hard at school might work well in a completely different setting. It will also mean giving thought to how an incentive is structured and framed. Should you reward the ultimate goal (grades), or behaviours that help you or others get there (attendance, behaviour and homework), and should you use monetary or non-monetary rewards? And if you decide to use financial incentives, you may want to consider whether to frame a reward as 'gaining' £80, or setting £80 aside and taking it away from the person who fails to achieve the objective in question. These are identical rewards, but bite in very different ways.

So it's clear that how we design and set a reward mechanism is of crucial importance to how effective it is likely to be at encouraging us to achieve our goals. And here, more than ever, the details that matter. We will outline two different but complementary ways of using rewards – one focused on achieving the overall objective and the other on rewarding the behaviours that will help you get there. We will also highlight the potential pitfalls to avoid when using rewards. So, the three lessons for setting rewards to encourage you to achieve your goals are:

- **Put something meaningful at stake.** Link achieving your ultimate goal to a significant reward, and make it binding and enforceable.
- **Use small rewards to build good habits.** Motivate yourself

or others along the way by using smaller incentives linked to specific steps needed to achieve the overarching goal.

- **Beware of backfire effects.** Financial incentives can 'crowd out' your intrinsic motivations, so be careful that rewards (or penalties) don't undermine good intentions. You can do this by using different types of non-financial rewards.

Rule 1: Put something meaningful at stake

Dean Karlan is a Professor of Economics at Yale University, and one of our favourite behavioural scientists. This is because his studies not only reveal important insights into human behaviour, but demonstrate how they can be applied to achieving goals in real world settings. One of the most interesting of these studies, conducted with fellow behavioural scientists Jonathan Zinman and Xavier Giné from the World Bank, focuses on how financial incentives can be used to help achieve their personal goals and what some of the conditions might be to help make them effective.[2] In partnership with the Green Bank in the Philippines, they sought to test the effectiveness of getting smokers to put something at stake to help them quit smoking. After identifying a group of smokers who wanted to quit, the team randomly assigned some of them to a group who would be given the opportunity to open a bank account into which they would deposit money that would be forfeited if they failed to stop smoking. They called the programme 'Committed Action to Reduce and End Smoking' (CARES).

The CARES clients got to choose how much of their own money to put at stake, but they were encouraged to use the money they would normally have spent on cigarettes into the bank account. The average client made a deposit every two weeks and ended up committing 550 pesos (US $11) by the end of the six-month contract period. This was about 20 per cent of their monthly income, so these were big sums. There was another important feature of the accounts. The smokers who signed up for the CARES accounts were free to choose whether or not they wanted to take up the programme. But once they had decided to do so, they were required to sign binding contracts that would prevent them from backing out. Green Bank technicians were trained to test, using urine strips, whether anyone had been secretly taking a drag in between making deposits. Only a zero result counted as passing and if they failed to pass the urine test, all the money they had accumulated in their CARES accounts would be given to charity. In other words they'd lose up to six months of hard-earned cash for a single cigarette. If they passed, though, the successful quitters would get a nice windfall – and to top it all, they would have not been smoking for so long that they would be unlikely to have a craving to spend the cash on cigarettes.

Now, nicotine is an addictive substance, so if reward schemes like this can be shown to work in helping people quit smoking, we can be fairly confident that they can help us to achieve other kinds of goals too. And the scheme was effective. Very effective. Participants in the programme who had taken up the CARES accounts were more than 30 per cent more likely to pass the nicotine test than their compatriots who did not. Better still, the effects were long lasting. After twelve months, Karlan, Zinman and Giné conducted some surprise tests on the original participants and found that the CARES account holders were still much more likely not to be smoking than those who hadn't had the accounts.[3]

Before we all go charging off to set up for ourselves extravagant reward systems to help us achieve our goals, it may not surprise you to learn that the details matter. The good news is that there are four relatively straightforward lessons that will help you to set yourself an effective reward mechanism. The first of these is that you need to make sure that there is a straight line between the reward you set yourself and your overarching goal. In other words, your reward should only pay out when you've achieved your ultimate objective. The easiest way of doing this is to link your reward to the commitment you made in the previous chapter – your commitment should state what it is that you are committing to achieving and when. So if you want to lose weight, make sure that your reward pays out when you have reached the weight you have pledged to meet – no prizes for nearly getting there (though in the next section, we will see how we can build smaller reward mechanisms into our goal achievement on an ongoing basis – something which was present in the GCSE rewards study)!

The second, related element is that it needs to be a meaningful reward. No small trinkets for achieving your headline objective. As a group of behavioural scientists who have studied the effects of incentives upon people's behaviour have persuasively argued: 'Pay enough or don't pay at all'.[4] Indeed, Karlan himself understood this lesson when setting himself a personal goal for losing weight. After finishing his doctoral thesis, he and a friend decided that, if either of them failed to meet their weight-loss target they'd have to give the other half of their annual income! He decided to put a large sum of money at play not because he was a reckless gambler, but because he wanted to ensure that it would bite whenever he had the urge to head to the freezer for a tub of ice cream. Now, we don't think it's necessary or appropriate to put half your salary on the line if you are going to set yourself an incentive of this kind, but the broad point remains – that if you are going to use a financial reward, it has to be meaningful in the context in which it is set to be effective. A quick word of warning before we move on: do not assume that these rewards need to be financial. In the final section of this chapter we will explore in detail how and why financial incentives can backfire, and what some alternatives to cold, hard cash might be. But for now, it's enough to say that if you don't much care for the prize you have set yourself, it's unlikely to be a great source of motivation.

The third feature of a good reward is that it needs to be binding. You need to be certain that, if you succeed, it will pay out. This was the lesson Karlan learnt when setting his own weight-loss reward scheme. Karlan discovered that it was easy for him and his friend to rewrite the rules after they'd failed to start losing weight, especially as they had set the bar so high at half their salaries. They both realized that for their incentive to be effective, it would need to be binding. So they drew up a contract, which stated that any attempt by either of them to renegotiate the terms of the contract would result in immediate failure. In short, they'd have to pay up, and there would be no way of backing out of the arrangement. Karlan puts great store by this particular aspect of his scheme, which helped them both shed the pounds. In the quit-smoking accounts in the Philippines, no one was left in any doubt that the contracts were binding – their money was being held by the bank and everyone was clear that if they failed to pass a urine test, it would be forfeited. And in the school exam scheme, everyone participating had faith that the schools would pay out once it was in place.

If you want to make your reward binding, the best and simplest way of doing so is to call on the services of your commitment referee. In the 'Commit' chapter, we saw how Rory asked Owain to act as his commitment referee to help him exercise more. One of Owain's key roles was to help Rory set the terms of his reward (or in this case his penalty: wearing an Arsenal shirt if he failed to meet his exercise goals) and it was Owain's job to determine whether or not Rory had failed to meet his goal and warranted being punished. So, when you are setting yourself a reward, do it in partnership with your commitment referee and ask them to enforce the terms of your binding commitment, which will include determining whether or not you deserve the rewards you have set yourself.

The fourth and final aspect of a good incentive is much more subtle and goes to the heart of one of the most celebrated findings in the behavioural science literature. It is that human beings care much more about losing something than they do about gaining something of an equivalent size.[5] There's a really simple way of testing yourself when it comes to what is referred to as 'loss aversion'. Think about how you would feel if you were walking along the street and you found a crisp £20 note lying on the floor. There's no way of returning it to its rightful owner, so you put it in your pocket, feeling pretty happy about just having unexpectedly acquired a small windfall. Now think about how you would feel if you went out for the day and popped into a local shop to buy something, reached for your wallet and discovered that you'd lost £20. It was there earlier that day, but it's gone now. How much worse does this loss feel than the equivalent gain of £20 in the previous example? Most people would say that it feels much worse. Experiments have repeatedly shown that losses hurt us about twice as much as equivalent gains, and that we ascribe most value to things we already possess (something which behavioural scientists call the 'endowment effect'[6]). That's why, when you are setting your reward structure, you should think about how you can do so in a way that taps into loss aversion to maximize the power of the effect. This is why, in the GCSE exam study, the cash and the tickets were pre-loaded into pupils' accounts so that failure to show the requisite effort would result in their loss. And it's why, in the smoking cessation bank accounts, you locked away your money and then lost it if you failed to quit smoking. This was a greater motivator for people than thinking about the windfall at the end of the six-month programme. So when you are setting your reward, think about how you can put something at stake that results in you losing something if you fail.

We hope to have demonstrated not only that rewards can be a powerful tool for achieving your overall goal, but also the details in how you set your incentives are incredibly important and tricky to get right. If you follow these four simple elements – link the reward to your ultimate objective; make it meaningful; make it binding; and use loss aversion – your reward will likely spur you to your goal more quickly. This section has been about your overarching objective – the final goal you want to meet. In the next section, we will look at how we can build smaller rewards into each of the 'chunks' of the activities that ultimately lead to our goal.

Rule 2: Use small rewards to build good habits

Timboon is a small town in Victoria, Australia, not that far from Melbourne. Timboon suffers from a problem it shares with towns across Australia and throughout the Western world: its citizens are getting fatter. They're also becoming less active than they once were. It was for this reason that the Behavioural Insights Team partnered with VicHealth, the organization tasked with promoting the good health of people in the Australian state of Victoria, to understand what could be done to help reduce obesity in the region. Through this partnership, we teamed up with Timboon and District Healthcare Services to see if we could increase levels of physical activity in the town. Being the kind of organization that likes to live by its own principles, Timboon and District Healthcare Services suggested that we start with its own staff – part of a growing recognition among employers that physical activity is a key driver of their staff's wellbeing. They already had a promising workplace health initiative, in which staff were given Fitbit devices and encouraged to hit 10,000 steps a day. But the data showed that, while there were decent levels of engagement, the number of steps, and of calories that people were burning, was starting to drop. So Alex Gyani, a senior member of the Behavioural Insights Team's Australian office, started a project with Tania Leishman, the Timboon Health Promotion Officer, to see if they could help encourage people to make more sustained changes in their behaviour. They knew that using big rewards could help staff achieve a longer-term objective, but they were also aware that smaller, more frequent rewards can be just as powerful at helping to build up daily habits.

So Alex and Tania decided to put this idea into action. They wanted a reward that was appealing enough to help kick-start the motivation of staff. But it had to be affordable for the organization. In the end they agreed on something that went with the grain of the programme, while also giving people a luxurious treat: a $50 massage voucher if the whole team walked an additional 2,500 steps per day (compared to their historical average) on five out of seven days of the week. In this way, the rewards were specifically focused on encouraging each person to walk a little more each day, rather than on a generic target of 10,000 steps a day, which some people were already meeting. Crucially they were also focused on rewarding daily behaviours and prompting staff to help encourage each other.

After the programme was put in place, Alex and Tania stepped back and waited for the data to come in. This showed that the reward scheme had a big effect, increasing the number of steps people were taking by over 2,100 every week and significantly increasing the calories they burnt through the week. Best of all, it seemed to have the greatest effect on those who needed it most: less physically active people were the ones who showed the biggest weekly improvements.

In the previous section, we saw how rewards can be really effective at helping us to stay on track with our headline objective. The rewards in these instances need to be sufficiently large to keep you motivated over a long period of time. But the Timboon scheme illustrates a different principle and supports another core tenet of the *thinking small* approach. Alongside your ultimate goal, you will have broken your goal down into a set of smaller 'chunks'. And it can be helpful to set yourself smaller rewards that are linked to each of these chunks, all the while ensuring, of course, that these separate activities are connected to achieving your ultimate goal. The chunks or activities that you reward can become more stretching over time (this is known as 'shaping'). For example, if you want to encourage your child to clean their room, you may want to first reward them for cleaning up one toy, the next time for cleaning up five toys, and so on. The great thing about these kinds of rewards, all of which should be small 'well dones' rather than big windfalls, is that they can help you to build up habitual behaviours, linked to your daily routine (the subject of the 'Plan' chapter). Such rewards are likely to be most helpful in those day-to-day situations when you know you probably should be doing something, but are struggling to get around to it. The reward in these instances can provide you with that little extra bit of a reason for following through, particularly if you felt the need to give yourself an additional incentive to get things moving in the first place.

These kinds of smaller, more regular rewards have been studied in one of the trickiest areas of behavioural change: trying to get kids to eat more fruit and vegetables. As any parent knows, this is a far from straightforward task, so numerous researchers have sought to discover what kinds of things might motivate children to eat more healthily. In one of the biggest studies of its kind, a group of researchers took on the challenge of devising new ways of encouraging thousands of children across forty elementary schools in Utah to eat more healthily. They wanted to see whether small rewards would help encourage children to eat more fruit and vegetables. Not just once or twice. But as a choice they would actively make in the future by turning their fruit and vegetable choices into long-term habits. The idea was a simple one. Whenever a pupil ate at least one serving of fruit or vegetables, they would receive a small reward in the form of a special token. The tokens had a real value (25 cents), but could only be redeemed in the school store, school carnival or book fair, so as to avoid any of the rewards for healthy eating being spent on cakes and chocolate. The researchers decided to run two variants of the programme: in some schools, the daily rewards were given for three weeks, and then stopped; in other schools, the rewards were offered for a total of five weeks.[7]

Before the study was run, it was far from clear how well the small reward scheme would work. It is notoriously difficult to get children to eat broccoli and peas when pizza and chips are available. But the rewards turned out to be incredibly effective. They led to a doubling in the number of children eating at least one serving of fruit and vegetables every day. Intriguingly, though, this wasn't the main point of this particular study. The main question was what would happen *after* the incentives were removed. As we saw in the 'Plan' chapter, repeating the same actions (asking for a portion of fruit or vegetables with your lunch) in response to the same cues (standing in line and being asked what you want to eat) helps to create habits that will over time make it easier to achieve your goal. This was one of the reasons that the researchers chose to run the programme for different lengths of time – to see whether a longer period of rewards (five weeks) might help to sustain the eating habits to a greater extent than the shorter programme (three weeks). So when the researchers went back two months later they were delighted to find that both the short and the long programme had strong, sustained effects. The effects of the five-week programme, however, were much more impressive. Kids who'd received the rewards over a longer period were seeing increases in fruit and vegetable consumption that were twice as big as those in the shorter programme. It seemed that the repetition of the scheme over a longer period of time in the five-week scheme had helped to ingrain these habits more deeply. This reinforces evidence that using more rewards over a longer period of time will increase the likelihood that the behaviour will be sustained after the rewards stop.

The rewards at the heart of this schools eating programme were given out whenever the kids had eaten sufficient quantities of fruit and vegetables. But one of the other features of many small reward programmes, including the one we put in place in Timboon, was that there was an element of competition about it. In fact, any scheme that encourages groups of people to collect rewards over an extended period of time is ripe for introducing some form of competition. 'Gamifying' your goal in this way through rewards and competition is being looked at seriously not only by app developers, but policymakers and companies around the world. We think that there is huge potential for gamifying your goal, whether it's a personal or a work-related challenge you're seeking to achieve.

Let's look at what happened, for example, when some of the core tenets of the Utah school study were tried in English schools, but with a stronger focus on competition and 'gamification'. In this study, kids received stickers rather than tokens for choosing fruit and vegetables at lunchtime. At the end of the week, pupils who'd gained at least four stickers could choose a small reward (such as a toy) from a special box. The researchers found that these small rewards helped to encourage the children to eat more fruit and vegetables, as it did in the Utah study. But when they introduced an element of competition – by placing the kids in groups of four and allowing only those with the highest numbers of stickers to choose a reward – it increased fruit and vegetable consumption by three times as much.[8]

So if you can, when you are setting your own goal, or if you are designing a reward programme to motivate other people, think about how you can gamify the goal, by linking the achieving of 'chunks' to rewards and then getting people and teams to compete against each other. These smaller rewards along the way will help you build up good habits.

The first two sections of this chapter have been about how we can put in place rewards to motivate us. But we haven't yet fully explored some of the complexities in using rewards, including how they can backfire if you set them incorrectly; the subject of the final section.

Rule 3: Beware of backfire effects

In the early 1990s, the Swiss government was intending to build two repositories to store nuclear waste. Two communities, located in central Switzerland, had been designated as potential sites. As might have been expected, it was an issue about which Swiss citizens, used to participating in referenda on questions of local importance, had strong views. This gave two academics, Bruno Frey and Felix Oberholzer-Gee, an idea for an intriguing research project. They contacted two-thirds of the households in the affected areas and asked the local residents whether they would be willing to permit the construction of a nuclear waste repository in their community. To the surprise of many at the time, just over half of the respondents said yes. This despite the fact that many of them were genuinely concerned about the potential negative consequences. Nearly 40 per cent of all respondents, for example, believed that there were considerable risks of serious accidents – not something that you'd want to happen anywhere near your home.[9] The residents, though, seemed to recognize that the facilities would have to go somewhere, and that alongside the concerns they had over potential accidents they also had civic duties as Swiss citizens.

Frey and Oberholzer-Gee then asked a slightly different set of questions. They wanted to know how many people would be willing to accept the waste facilities if they were also offered financial compensation. The compensation varied from $2,175 to $6,525 per individual, per year. With this payment added to their sense of civic duty, you might have thought that the citizens now had even more reason to say yes. They were being offered money to add to their underlying motivations. But while over 50 per cent of the respondents said yes without any cash incentive, when the compensation was offered, the acceptance levels plummeted. Suddenly only a quarter of respondents were prepared to accept the facilities. And just as interestingly, the amount of money – whether it was just over $2,000 or more than $6,000 – didn't have any bearing on people's views.

What was going on? Far from supplementing the residents' intrinsic motivation, it seemed that the offer of cash had turned what was previously a moral duty into a financial transaction. And the money on offer, even at $6,000, wasn't high enough to compensate for the perceived risks. Findings like these have often puzzled classical economists, who might assume that offering an additional payment would only have the effect of increasing the benefits to the individual and therefore increasing the positive response rates. But behavioural scientists no longer find these results particularly surprising. There are now hundreds of illustrations of this phenomenon, but again the context and details are important. For example, Richard Titmuss's work famously indicated that paying people to donate blood would negatively effect their willingness to do so. But more recent work by Bob Slonim challenges this assumption. His experiments indicate that the way these rewards are framed is important, and well-designed incentive schemes can in fact increase donation rates.[10] In short, putting up a monetary reward for your goal, which you should have intrinsic motivation to achieve anyway, may not always be a good idea and could even undermine your efforts if not designed carefully.

One of the most famous experiments that shows how easy it is for financial incentives to backfire was conducted by Uri Gneezy in Israel, where 'donation days' take place every year. Each of these days is devoted to a particular society that collects donations from the public for a charitable cause – like cancer research or helping disadvantaged children. In what is a well-established practice, high-school students go in pairs from door to door to collect the donations. What Gneezy wanted to know was whether or not these students would collect more money when they themselves had a financial incentive to go alongside their underlying motivations to help these good causes. So he set up a trial in which the high-school students were split into three very different groups. The students in the first group were given a speech in which they were told about the importance of the donations they were about to collect. They were also told that the results would be published, so that the amount collected by each pair would become public knowledge. The second group were given the same speech, but they were also given a small incentive: each pair would get to keep 1 per cent of the total amount they collected. The third group were given a much larger incentive of 10 per cent.

So what do you think happened? Well, the biggest collections were made by those who received no financial incentive, closely followed by the group with the large incentive of 10 per cent. But the group that were given the speech together with a small incentive collected a far smaller amount of money – 36 per cent less. Collecting money for charity has an intrinsic motivation for people, so the introduction of a small monetary reward displaced this with an extrinsic reward, which was far less powerful than the pull of helping out a good cause. Just like in Switzerland, it seemed that far from helping to motivate people, the incentive had put people off. It had displaced the students' intrinsic motivation.

Before we move on, we should be mindful of the central message here, which many commentators misinterpret to mean that financial incentives do not work. This is how many people misrepresent perhaps the most celebrated study that's been conducted in this area, which looked at what happened when parents started being fined for turning up late to pick up their kids from childcare. The study, also conducted by Uri Gneezy and Aldo Rustichini, famously showed that the fines backfired: they doubled the number of parents who turned up late, for the same reason that Swiss citizens didn't want to be paid to host nuclear facilities.[11] In this case, the moral duty of turning up on time to support the hard-working childcare assistants had been turned into a financial transaction. Suddenly it was OK to turn up late – the fine had replaced the moral obligation. But Gneezy and Rustichini's broader point was not that fines do not work. It was that, if you are going to use a financial reward or penalty, you need to think hard about the level at which to set the price, especially when people already have an intrinsic motivation to 'do the right thing'. So this is why, in the first section of this chapter, we emphasized that whatever you put at stake has to be sufficiently large to bite. So if you are going to use financial incentives, make them meaningful. Of course if you set the reward too high it may not be cost effective, or worse, it may even encourage cheating, dishonesty or reduce performance.[11]

An alternative approach, which we think is likely to be more appropriate for most people setting a goal which they should already have an intrinsic motivation to achieve, is to avoid using straight, cash rewards. In line with the broader *think small* principles, we have devised three different ways in which you can do this. The first is to reframe the cash reward so that it is focused not on the money, but on the thing that is being purchased. This is what some clever researchers effectively did in a scheme designed to incentivize Singaporean taxi drivers to exercise more. Some people were offered a $100 cash reward, but this was far less effective than the alternative reward of paying for the driver's taxi lease for a day.[12] Why should we be surprised by this? Well, the cost of the lease was $100 a day. To apply this to your own goal, focus on the things that you would really like to do to celebrate achieving your ultimate objective. But instead of setting a cash reward for yourself, focus on the thing that your cash will buy you. It might be a holiday that you've always intended to go on. It could involve throwing the mother of all parties. Or it might be treating yourself to a season pass to a cinema, or your favourite sports team. When you are thinking about what this reward should be, keep in mind the lessons from the 'Set' chapter: that buying 'experiences' rather than physical products, extending social relationships, and giving time and money to others are all more likely to improve your wellbeing than physical products. Studies have shown, for example, that employees who had donations made to a charity on their behalf were happier and more satisfied than those who were given the money to spend on themselves.[13]

The second principle is a close relative of the first, and is particularly appropriate for setting rewards for *other people*. This is to abandon the idea of paying for things completely and to think about things that money cannot buy. Public bodies, for example, should think more about the things they have access to that might offer much stronger value to someone than cash (the fallback option). Imagine the lure of being the only person who is allowed to park where it is usually forbidden for a year; or to have lunch with an individual for whom you have a particular admiration (the premise behind a lot of money-raising auctions). When the city of Oslo wanted to get more people to start buying electric vehicles, for example, they allowed anyone driving one to use the bus lanes. Not only did this increase the number of electric vehicles purchased, it also made them more visible too – suddenly it was very apparent how many other people were in environmentally friendly rides. At the Behavioural Insights Team, we devised a small-scale version of this 'money can't buy' principle with one of the founding members of the team, Simon Ruda. Every year we have specially made pens produced at Christmas, embossed with the Behavioural Insights Team logo, the initials of the recipient, and the year. The equivalent worth of these pens is relatively small, but everyone attaches great value to them – far beyond what they cost to produce. So if you're

Whereas all the other golden rules in this book have been about a positive step that you can take to achieve your goal, this one has primarily focused on how things could go wrong. It is possible for reward mechanisms to backfire if they are set inappropriately. But with a few, simple techniques and a bit of thought, it's possible to set yourself rewards that will help to spur you towards your goal.

This chapter has been about putting in place rewards to help you or others achieve certain goals. But we've seen that it's not as simple as we might assume. You should ensure that any overarching reward is meaningful by focusing on four key principles: directly link the reward (or sanction) to your overarching goal; make sure it's sufficiently meaningful to you that you really care about the outcome; ensure that it is binding; and think about setting it up so that you stand to lose (rather than gain) something. But alongside a big reward for achieving your ultimate goal, you should consider supplementing this with smaller incentives linked to specific 'chunks' of activities. The idea here is to be able to put in place mechanisms that offer you frequent equivalents of the pat-on-the-back, which can help to encourage the formation of good habits. Finally, we highlighted that you should be aware of the potential for straight financial incentives to undermine your intrinsic motivation. Thankfully, there are lots of ways to avoid this happening – for example, by framing your incentives carefully, rewarding yourself with experiences instead of money, or even creating 'anti-incentives'.

5

SHARE

Andy is one of the Behavioural Insights Team's excellent recent hires. He comes from Grimsby where he had a dedicated group of friends, all of whom smoked. Andy didn't really think of himself as a smoker at the time, but when others lit up, he did too. He was your archetypal 'social smoker'. When he moved up to Bristol to go to university, a similar pattern emerged. Many of his new student friends were smokers, and when they would light up on a night out, Andy would smoke too. The pattern continued for the next couple of years – Andy would rarely smoke when others around him weren't also having a cigarette. Then, in his final year, the pattern began to change. He got involved in student politics and during the 2010 General Election campaign Andy spent much of his time in the headquarters of one of the local political parties. Almost everyone else on the campaign was a smoker and they regularly took cigarette breaks throughout the day to help de-stress from the hustle and bustle associated with it. When they did, Andy would join them. But now he'd occasionally initiate the breaks too. He started to realize that the social smoking he'd engaged in in Grimsby and then in his student days at Bristol, generally in the evenings, was turning into more regular daytime affairs. He had, in short, become a fully fledged nicotine addict. It felt as though he had slipped into it by stealth. 'You wake up one morning, reach for a cigarette and suddenly you realize you're not a social smoker any more,' Andy later reflected. 'Suddenly you're an actual smoker.'

Then one day, everything changed. Andy met Nicola and they fell in love. The trouble was that Nicola wasn't a smoker. In fact, she hated smoking. She hated the way it turned your teeth yellow and made your clothes stink, and she was pretty sure that she didn't want to be settling down with anyone who was prepared to slowly kill themselves by continuing to smoke. So she made it abundantly clear to Andy that if he wanted to take her to be his lawfully wedded wife, he'd need to quit. This would have been a fairly daunting prospect for most people. Nicotine, after all, is a highly addictive substance. But Andy was armed with knowledge from behavioural science research that gave him good reason to be confident. So he took up Nicola's stringent condition for marriage and agreed to quit smoking.

The reason for Andy's confidence was his understanding of the social component of goal achievement. He recognized the influence of others upon him, both in causing him to smoke in the first place, and in potentially helping him to quit. So Andy accepted his bride-to-be's quit-smoking condition not just because he was in love (though that of course played a big part), but because he knew that he could rely upon Nicola to help him achieve his goal. New research strongly backed up Andy's hypothesis. When one spouse stops smoking, the other spouse is 67 per cent less likely to smoke.[1] However, the story doesn't end there. Another important factor at play here was the fact that he and Nicola planned to move out of Bristol, away from the social networks that he was embedded within and that would otherwise have had a big effect upon his ability to quit. Andy was also aware of new findings showing the strong influence of the social networks you are embedded within. So much so that if your friend's friend's friend smokes, you are more likely to smoke too.[2] So Andy knew that extracting himself from his social networks in Bristol and Grimsby would make it far easier to quit, just as these very same networks had been partly responsible for him taking up tobacco in the first place. Two years on, and it looks like Andy was right to be confident. He hasn't had a cigarette since moving out of Bristol. The following year, he and Nicola got married and they are very happy with their new, smokeless life together.

This chapter, then, is about how we can draw on the powerful influence of those around us to help us to achieve our goals. Sharing a goal is a great way of helping to keep motivated and on track, but in our personal lives it has become an under-used tactic because we tend to think of goals as *individual* betterment projects. Similarly, in our work lives, and certainly in government policy, we have historically ignored the social component of the projects or programmes we are putting in place, because we have adopted economic assumptions about the way that individuals maximize their own self-interest, without thinking about how important our social interactions are. As Richard Thaler – who as well as being a long-term advisor to the Behavioural Insights Team is also president of the American Economics Association – has put it: 'The purely economic man is indeed close to being a social moron.'[3] But before you continue reading, we want you to bear in mind one of the positive side effects of the power of social networks, which explains why we have decided to call this chapter 'Share'. If you ask a friend, family member or colleague to help you to do something, it will trigger within you (and them) a strong urge to give something back. To reciprocate. This urge is so strong that Darwin considered it the foundation stone of morality.[4] It's the same urge you feel to give something back when someone gives you a present, pays you a compliment or invites you round to theirs for dinner. So we hope that, alongside you seeking out the support of others to help you achieve your goals, you also take the opportunity to help others with theirs.

We are social animals.[5] We are influenced by what we think other people are doing, and what they think about us. Often unconsciously, and usually to a far greater extent than we realize. The three golden rules we encourage you to put in place to help use this social component to best effect are:

- **Ask for help.** You are more likely to achieve your goal if you get someone to help you. You may be surprised at how willing others will be to support you.
- **Tap into your social networks.** The networks we are embedded within have a profound effect on our behaviour. There are lots of ways you can draw on them to help you achieve your goals.
- **Use group power.** Band together with a large group of people trying to achieve the same goal, and you're likely to achieve more, faster, than you can by yourself.

Rule 1: Ask for help

Imagine you are in the following situation. You're in New York and you need to make a phone call, but your mobile phone is out of battery. It's pretty urgent, so you decide to approach strangers in the street to ask them if you can borrow their phone to make a call. What proportion of people do you think would say yes? Have a think before you consider a second situation. You're a student and you need to get to the gym, which you happen to know is where all students go for their compulsory physical education courses. So you stop another student in the street and ask them where the gym is. They point you in the right direction, but instead of stopping at that, you ask: 'Will you walk me there?' What proportion of people do you think might agree to this request? Again, pause for a moment and think about what you think the answer might be.

These were the scenarios devised by two researchers who wanted to know whether people were any good at estimating the likelihood that total strangers would comply with requests for help.[6] In the mobile phone study, participants predicted that 30 per cent of people would let them borrow their phone; and in the gym study, participants predicted that a paltry 14 per cent would agree to escort them to the gym. In both cases, however, close to half the people asked said yes (48 and 43 per cent of requests respectively).[7] Most people are really surprised when they hear how many people say yes when asked to do something that apparently comes with no benefits to the person saying yes. But these aren't just one-off findings. Vanessa Bohns, a psychologist from Cornell University, and colleagues have repeated these kinds of exercises with requests made of more than 14,000 strangers.[8] And they have found a similar pattern each time. We are overly pessimistic about our fellow humans beings' willingness to help us. In reality, people are often willing to help to a much greater extent than we imagine – around half the time they are asked.[9] The result of this is that most of us miss out on a big opportunity to benefit from one of the best sources of support for our goals that there is: the help of other people. Once we realize that close to 50 per cent of New Yorkers are willing to help someone whose mobile phone has run out of battery, imagine how many of those much closer to us are likely to be willing to help?

So the first, very simple, lesson is to ask others to help you achieve your goal. That's why at the Behavioural Insights Team, we often think about different ways of encouraging people to ask the question in the first place. One area in which we have taken this furthest has been in relation to education. Working with the Harvard academic Todd Rogers and Bristol University Professor Simon Burgess, the Behavioural Insights Team's Raj Chande devised a set of deceptively simple interventions that encouraged parents to help their children more directly with their education. Most parents want to help, but they often don't know where to start. They sometimes even feel a bit nervous that they won't be able to help – kids these days are learning all kinds of things that weren't part of their parents' syllabus. In this context, Raj often asks people to imagine a typical conversation with a parent and their son or daughter who has just come back from school. 'What homework do you have this weekend?' the parent asks, while awaiting the all-too-familiar reply: 'Not much, couple of things, the usual.' So the research team wanted to give parents just a little bit more information, affording them the ability to get more involved in their kids' education. Here's how it works. Around once a week parents would receive a text message from the school with different kinds of prompts in them. Some of these were advance notice of upcoming tests and others were updates on what their child had learnt in their science, maths and English lessons – with little prompts to encourage specific conversations about these topics. There's an example of one of these texts below. Take a look at it and imagine how it would change the conversation between a parent and their child.

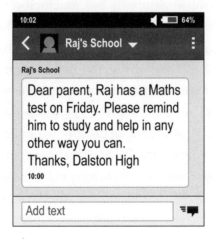

By this message being more specific, time-related and focused on something that a parent can actually do ('Please remind him to study'), most people guess that it would completely alter the parent–child dialogue. In this situation, for example, a parent might say: 'So you have a maths test on Friday. When are you going to revise? Can I help?' Though we may not know exactly what conversations do end up taking place, what we do know is the impact these kinds of interventions have on pupils' educational outcomes. The trial showed that these simple text messages improve educational outcomes by the equivalent of a month of learning – pretty remarkable for something that costs next to nothing to put into practice.[10] As well as being surprisingly effective, the texts are also popular. When asked if they would like to continue with the programme, the answer was invariably not just 'Yes', but 'Can you do it more frequently?' Even the pupils wanted more texts to be sent to their parents! And this has been borne out in follow-up studies in Further Education Colleges, in which the text messages are sent out on a weekly basis to help encourage pupils not to bunk off lessons and to achieve in their exams. In these settings we are finding even more powerful results. Weekly text messages sent to people whom the pupils nominate as their dedicated 'study supporter' are even helping to make sure that pupils show up at lessons – up to 11 per cent more often than those who don't get the texts.

These are the kind of findings that really excite the Education Endowment Foundation (EEF), an amazing organization that was set up with a £125 million founding grant from the Department for Education in 2011 to find out 'what works' in the classroom. Many of these studies, like the text message intervention, show the power of encouraging people to help each other. For example, one of the most effective changes that a head teacher can make is to get pupils to tutor *each other*.[11] 'Peer tutoring', which usually involves using pupils as one-to-one teachers, adds five additional months of educational progress to a pupil's education. Better still, it benefits both tutors and tutees, seeming to have the greatest impact on the lowest-attaining pupils.[12] It's very rare to find interventions like this – ones that don't cost a lot of money, that dramatically improve performance and that seem disproportionately to benefit those who need most help. So when we do find them, we should take them very seriously. And in this case, it's based on the very simple premise: people helping people to achieve their goals works.

We find similar results in all kinds of different areas. Smoking, alcohol-cessation and weight-loss programmes that provide peer support work better than those that do not.[13] If you're in any way sporty, you might have noticed that you are able to exercise faster or harder when you're working out with another person. These are both the result of the same phenomenon. We find it easier to stoke our motivation alongside other people, who have the ability to push us harder than we might do if we were working in isolation, and studies are showing just how effective this kind of practice can be. One group of researchers sought to test the effect of working with other people by asking a group of gym-goers to exercise on an exercise bike at 65 per cent of their heart rate on six separate days. The women were split into different groups. Some of them were told to exercise alone. Others were given a partner to exercise alongside. The mischievous twist was that the partner wasn't even real. It was in fact a virtual gym buddy, Skyping in for the session and, much as in the movie *Speed*, the gym buddy was actually on a filmed loop, so that they would always end up being able to outperform their real-life gym buddy. Those exercising with a buddy exercised for far longer than those exercising alone. It doubled the amount of time that participants exercised for.[14] So it seems that we can be more effective when we get other people to help us, especially if it helps to engender a sense of competition amongst friendly rivals.

The first lesson, then, in sharing your goal is the simplest and the easiest to put into practice: find someone who can help you achieve your goal. When you do find that person (or people), think about how you make your ask. Just like a parent receiving a text message from a school, your goal supporter will benefit from knowing how they can help you to achieve your goal. So focus your request on the specific actions you want someone to help with, together with when you want the support.[15]

Rule 2: Tap into your social network

For many of us, our first (and last) foray into construction and house building started with sets of coloured bricks. Lego is a company with a long heritage in toy making. It was founded back in 1932 by Ole Kirk Christiansen, a carpenter who designed a set of wooden toys that proved to be moderately successful in his native Denmark.[16] In the 1940s Christiansen spent two years of profits on something that no other toy manufacture had: a plastic injection-moulding machine. Over the next fifty years Lego sets proved to be a phenomenal success, and the company started making serious money. In the fifteen years from 1978, the company doubled in size every five years and by 1993 was generating some $1.2 billion in revenues. But not much more than a decade later, the company was on the brink of bankruptcy. In 2004 Lego posted its third annual loss in five years, and was reliant on loans from its controlling family members. How did such a successful business, with such a clear and popular product line, fall from grace? Many business school case studies of companies that have dramatically gone from world-beaters to basket cases focus on an inability to innovate in a changing world. Not so Lego. The generally accepted view is that, far from not innovating enough, the company had gone too far in the other direction: it had 'lost control of its innovation efforts'. It diversified too greatly – buying an 'intelligent toy' maker in California, opening an internet business in New York and a design studio in Milan. Some of the games devised in these projects had almost no construction element in them at all.[17]

The remarkable thing about Lego is not its sudden fall. It was the way that, over the next ten years, it managed to turn things around. By 2013, it had become the biggest toy manufacturer in the world, bigger than its arch-rivals Mattel and Hasbro, with a total company value approaching $15 billion. A new set of business school case studies are now being written to explain the return to form in the decade or so since its new CEO Jørgen Vig Knudstorp has been running the company. These will focus on a variety of factors. There was a lot of financial work to be done – getting debt and cash flow under control, and selling parts of the Lego empire that were deemed not to be essential to the core business. But one of the principal reasons given for the dramatic turnaround has been Lego's ability to harness the power of its legion of fans. The company managed to tap into the social networks that had built up around the brand, which had previously not been recognized as the huge potential asset that it was. And there was no better illustration of this than the launch of 'Lego Ideas', starting in Japan in 2008 and then taken global in 2011. The idea was both simple and ground-breaking. Rather than getting Lego employees to think up new product lines, why not get the customers who would ultimately want to buy them to make and suggest them? Better still, why not get these same people, self-selecting as ardent Lego fans, to help promote the products even before they go on sale? And that's exactly what Lego did.

Anyone can submit a Lego idea. All you need to do is create a model, take some photos of it, make a project plan and then upload it onto the Lego website.[18] The catch is that you then need to gather the support of 10,000 people over a two-year period. But this is at the heart of what remains a genius idea. Lego has managed to create a facility that helps it to determine whether or not an idea is likely to fly. In the past, they would have had to do a huge amount of product development, and then take a punt on a particular product without knowing for sure how popular it might be. But now they have a mechanism that tells them whether a product is likely to be successful before their employees even start getting involved. And sometimes this happens so quickly that Lego are able to spot instant bestsellers. When a Minecraft fan posted an idea for a set based on their favourite online game, they managed to get the 10,000 votes in two days. Six months later, Lego Minecraft Micro was in the shops and became an international bestseller.[19] Other examples include birds (blue jays, robins and hummingbirds), a Doctor Who set and a maze made entirely out of Lego bricks. But one of the other things that makes Lego Ideas so appealing to its legion of followers is that the company intuitively seems to understand the reciprocal nature of the relationship. They don't just take the ideas and then commercialize them. They allow the person who came up with the idea to have input into the final sets alongside professional designers. The individual is also featured in the final product, and even receives a royalty on the sales.

Lego is by no means the only company that is tapping into the power of social networks to drive innovation and customer service. From Apple support communities where customers help solve each other's issues to Lay's crisps 2013 'Do us a Flavour' campaign, which received more than 14 million flavour ideas submitted by the public,[20] companies around the world are using social networks to power innovation and efficiencies. And it's not only companies and organizations that can use these networks. It is hard to exaggerate the power that the social networks we are embedded within have upon our daily lives. Behavioural research is starting to show this in new and stark ways. At the start of this chapter, we saw, in the example of Andy and his attempts to quit smoking, how profound the effect of social networks can be. But similar effects are now being unearthed in relation to many of the most pressing issues facing people in developed countries. Take obesity, for example. We might think about the process of becoming obese as being an intensely personal one. After all, it's up to you how much you eat and how much you exercise. But at the same time, anyone who's travelled to other countries knows that obesity rates differ widely. And one of the reasons for this is the widespread effect that the social networks we are embedded within have upon us. One of the most sophisticated analyses of this phenomenon has been conducted by Nicholas Christakis and James Fowler, who looked at obesity in over 12,000 people who underwent repeated weight measurement between 1971 and 2003. These facts alone make the study pretty amazing – the breadth and depth of the data available enabled them to look at social networking effects on an unprecedented scale. Their findings were very similar to those that Andy encountered in relation to smoking. Far from being a purely personal phenomenon, obesity in fact travels through social networks. They found that the risk of obesity in people who were directly connected to someone who was obese was about 45 per cent higher than it would have been in a randomly selected network.

When Grant used a Reciprocity Ring with a group of his students, he found that they came up with lots of surprising offers of support, despite their initial scepticism. For example, one of his students was a theme park enthusiast who explained that his dream was one day to run an amusement park chain named Six Flags. It turned out that another classmate had a connection with the former CEO and managed to connect them to each other. When the Behavioural Insights Team got everyone to gather in a circle and encouraged people to make requests for support through their social networks, it resulted in tens of offers of help from colleagues in all kinds of different areas. One colleague announced – much to everyone's surprise – that they wanted to learn how to fly. Did anyone have any connections? Well, it turned out that lots of people knew others who might be able to help: from a government official who originally trained with the Royal Air Force, to a commercial pilot who'd recently earned their stripes. Just like the study on obesity, you will be surprised by how far and wide your social network reaches, and you shouldn't be afraid to use it to help you achieve your goal.

There are lots of other ways in which you can tap into your own and other people's social networks. In fact, a growing range of the Behavioural Insights Team's results focus on what we call 'network nudges', in which we don't just focus on how we can encourage someone to change their behaviour, but encourage someone to encourage *someone else* to change their behaviour. This is exactly what the Behavioural Insights Team's head of research, Michael Sanders, tested when he was devising new ways of encouraging investment bankers to donate a day of their (ample) salary to good causes. In the original studies, Michael had found that hard-nosed investment bankers were twice as likely to

A Behavioural Insights Team Reciprocity Ring in action.

donate when they had been given a pot of sweets on the way into work by the fundraisers – the value of which was one thousand times lower than what they ultimately gave. That's reciprocity in action. But over time, Michael found that the effect wore off. Giving sweets to the same investment banker who gave last year still results in higher donation rates, but not as high as the year before. So the following year, rather than asking those investment bankers to give again, he asked them instead to reach out to colleagues and encourage them to donate. It was one of the most effective interventions we had ever come across to get people to support charitable causes, resulting in a deluge of donations. Donation rates jumped fourfold when Michael got investment bankers, famed for their individual pursuit of self-interest, to tap into their social networks at work.

The emergence of online social networks in the twenty-first century – Facebook, Twitter, Instagram etc. – has transformed our everyday ability to make use of those we're connected with in ways that we wouldn't have previously imagined possible. The challenge is no longer whether it's possible to tap into our social networks. It's how to structure these activities so that they can be channelled positively, to help us achieve our goals.

Rule 3: Use group power

In the weeks running up to February, you can feel the excitement start to build in the Behavioural Insights Team's offices around the world. In the London office, our finance manager Oliver normally starts to prepare the chin-up bar in the storeroom, for what will be a month of activity during the cold British winter. The Behavioural Insights Team's chief executive David Halpern – once famous for his ability to do one-arm chin-ups – starts warming up his arm. The already well-built Hugo, who leads some of our biggest health programmes, starts readying himself for an extra-hard month of exercise. Ariella, not renowned for her exercise regime, dusts off her running shoes. In Sydney, Guglielmo, Ed and Ravi start planning activities for the Australian sunshine – touch rugby, rounders and group workouts. In Singapore, preparations are being laid for some intense Zumba classes, drawing in as many participants as possible. And the newly established New York office is just beginning to realize that everyone else really means business. For during February, the Behavioural Insights Team's offices of the world compete against each other for the increasingly prestigious title of FitFeb champions.

It started a few years back, just after Rory had moved to Sydney, when the team he helped set up inside the New South Wales government threw down the gauntlet by challenging the London office to a series of fitness-related feats. Now, every February, each of the teams competes against one another to accumulate 'FitFeb' points – which can only be obtained by undertaking a series of fitness and healthy-eating challenges. You get points for various healthy behaviours, such as a point for every twenty minutes of exercise, and for every day you go without consuming alcohol. You also get bonus points for undertaking weekly challenges, like reconstructing an archetypally unhealthy meal into something nutritious. For example, one intrepid member of the Singaporean team managed to create a healthy alternative to fried egg and chips, using yoghurt, tinned peaches and apples. I'm sure you'll agree that the results look pretty appetizing.

It would be easy for a competition of this kind to backfire through being set up in the wrong way: by pitting individual against individual. In behavioural terms, the results would be fairly predictable: it would probably result in those who already do a lot of exercise really going for it, while the majority of their more leisurely colleagues put their feet up. But setting up the scoring system in a way that enables participants to gain points as individuals, but only to win as a team, encourages an entirely different set of behaviours. Suddenly, there is an incentive to encourage lagging colleagues to get involved, this being accentuated by each individual receiving more points for exercising with colleagues (double points for doing that) or organizing an office workout (just five minutes of this a day earns everyone in the office a point). It's amazing to see how socially difficult it is *not* to join an office workout in which everyone else is taking part. Of course, the points system is not without its flaws. In 2016 the London office deliberately timed a team ski trip to coincide with FitFeb, resulting in hundreds of extra points for five-hour exercise sessions. But more often than not the effects are most pronounced for those who would not have otherwise done a lot of exercise, as they are actively encouraged by their colleagues to get involved.

It is, perhaps, not that surprising to learn that human beings often work better together towards a goal as a group than when they work individually. After all, if you spend a moment thinking about humanity's greatest achievements, they almost invariably required large groups of people to collaborate. The famous story of John F. Kennedy asking a broom-carrying janitor at the NASA space centre in 1962 what he was doing illustrates the principle nicely. 'Well, Mr President,' he is reported to have said, 'I'm helping put a man on the moon.' We wouldn't be able to achieve such great feats without working together as a team. But too often we think about goals as individual activities, pursued in isolation from other people, despite the fact that in most areas of our working life, working in groups is the norm. And the evidence backs up this basic intuition. Take smoking, for example. If you look at smoking rates across an overall population, the total numbers of individuals and groups of smokers has declined, whilst the size of the groups of smokers remains roughly the same.[22] This at first appears to be paradoxical. If the overall population of smokers decreases, you'd expect the average size of the groups of smokers to decline too. Unless, of course, people quit together in groups. Then you would expect the group sizes to remain roughly constant, but for the number of groups to decline – and that's exactly what is happening.[23] People are giving up smoking not as individuals, but collectively in groups. Yet smokers rarely start by thinking about how to draw on the group dynamic from the outset to help them to achieve their goal.

This seems to be borne out in all kinds of other areas that will be relevant to various goals, especially when our natural instincts might be to try to achieve these alone. Take weight-loss programmes. Some of the most successful of these encourage participants to work together to lose weight, rather than simply attempting this by themselves. Probably the most famous example is the Weight Watchers programme. In one of the studies of the programme, which focused on 772 overweight individuals, people in the Weight Watchers group lost twice as much weight (5.06 kg) as those individuals who were not working together as part of a group (2.25 kg).[24] We see similar effects in completely different areas. Take savings, an area that you might think would not be particularly susceptible to the group dynamic. One of our favourite studies sought to test the effect of encouraging people to form groups of fellow savers, in which they set savings goals and then agreed to have them publicly announced and monitored (in other words, the group dynamic was combined with commitments and feedback). Researchers then looked at whether people in these groups would save more money than those saving alone, some of whom were also given the added incentive of a much higher interest rate (5 per cent instead of a baseline of 0.3 per cent). The group savings scheme doubled the amount that people deposited, while the higher saving rate did almost nothing.[25]

When we think about working together as a group, we normally envisage everyone mucking in together in the same location. But in an increasingly online and interconnected world, we can often now draw on virtual networks and groups of people. This is particularly true in our professional lives and for work-related goals. Indeed, at the Behavioural Insights Team, we have also become interested in growing evidence showing how powerful the decisions formed by groups of people can be. If they are correctly organized, people acting together can be smarter than experts acting alone. The idea was brilliantly used by Francis Galton in 1906, who became fascinated by the outcome of a weight-judging competition at the West of England Fat Stock and Poultry Exhibition. Some 800 people decided to pay the 6d entry fee to take a guess at the weight of a 'slaughtered and "dressed"' ox. As Galton explained, those guessing included some experts – farmers and butchers – but also plenty of ordinary people who fancied their chances. Galton wasn't interested in the competition, so much as in whether the collective guesses of the group would be close to the real weight of the ox. So he was surprised to find that, when it came to guessing the weight of farm animals, the group seemed to be incredibly good. 'It appears then, in this particular instance, that the *vox populi* [voice of the people] is correct to within 1 per cent of the real value.' At this particular moment in Britain's history, when the right to vote for men still required them to own certain forms of property, Galton was interested in what the effect of opening up the vote would mean for decision making. He concluded that the result seemed 'more creditable to the trustworthiness of a democratic judgment than might have been expected'.[26]

Some have used Galton's observations, and those of subsequent researchers, to conclude that the 'crowd' is always smarter than the individual. But it won't surprise you to learn that the research throws up a more subtle interpretation of when a large group of people comes up with more accurate results than if one were to rely on the individual opinions of experts alone. First, you need a diversity of opinions – for example, if you are predicting whether inflation will go up, you don't just want a group of economists, but also small business owners and financially stretched single parents. Research has shown that the collective predictions of these three types of people will be more accurate than when relying on the economist alone.[27] Each of them is able to draw on different sets of knowledge and experience. Importantly, though, the predictions of these people need to be made independently of each other – the business people shouldn't discuss their views with the economists or single parents first. Further, there obviously needs to be some way of aggregating views, to avoid the problem of simply having lots of disparate opinions about the question at hand.[28] When these conditions hold, there are very few experts who will outperform the group.[29]

Interestingly, diversity seems also to improve the performance of small groups. The excellent British author and commentator Tim Harford has recently argued that while people tend to prefer to work with friends or people they know well, introducing a stranger can improve overall performance.[30] So when putting teams together at work, you may want to consider deliberately combining people with different skills and backgrounds.

At the Behavioural Insights Team, we're drawing on these very principles to help achieve our organizational goals – based on this same idea that working together as a group is a good idea, but that how you do so matters a lot. When we brainstorm ideas, for example, to avoid 'groupthink' we often use online tools to ask individuals to draw on their own knowledge and expertise to come up with new ideas in isolation from one another before they are aggregated together.[31] When we finalize data analysis and reports, we ask people from outside the project team to undertake quality assurance and provide critical support and challenge. And when we started to devise our new recruitment practices, we developed an online platform which helps us draw on the power of the group to help us make our hiring decisions. The platform is called Applied, and starts by requiring the hiring manager to select a diverse range of people to conduct the initial sift. For example, we find that junior members of staff will spot different things (is this person going to be a good manager?) than their more senior colleagues identify (is this person going to deliver high-quality analysis?). These individuals then look at responses to questions independently of one another. The people doing the marking have no knowledge of whose scores they are marking and there is no conferring between individual sifters. The online platform then aggregates all of the sifters' responses, and allows the hiring manager to decide how many people to take through to the next stage. We've conducted a huge amount of analysis using the Applied platform, and have found that it radically changes our hiring decisions. When we ran an experiment on our recent graduate recruitment round (in which candidates went through a traditional sift and through Applied at the same time, so that we could see which worked best at finding the candidates we were looking for), we found that 60 per cent of the people we eventually hired would never have made it through the traditional sift.

What these examples show is that, while we usually think of our goals as personal to us, we're much more likely to achieve them if we work with other people. This might be as part of a team, working together towards a shared common goal. Or it might be drawing on the collective wisdom of the group in order to help us make better decisions.

It is often said that a 'problem shared is a problem halved' and the same can be said for achieving our goals. But too often, we keep them to ourselves, and consider them to be personal betterment projects rather than things that other people can help us with. In fact, the opposite is true. Other people play a vital role in helping us to achieve our goals and this chapter has shown three ways in which we can share our objectives with others to great effect. The simplest thing to do is to ask others for help. You'll be surprised by how willing others are to support you, and how much *they* get out of it. But you can get even further by tapping into your social networks. Whether you like it or not, your friends, family and colleagues will already be having a major influence upon your life, but you might not have thought before about how you can use the reach of that to help you achieve your goals. Again, you should remember that this isn't just about you – asking others to support your goal will also give you the opportunity to support others. Finally, we saw that you can have an even stronger impact if you work together with others as part of a group. This might be a group with a shared goal (losing weight, saving money, a team at work), or a group whose collective wisdom we harness to improve the decisions we take along the way. Whichever method you use, underlying the 'share' principle is the fact that human beings are social animals. And when we recognize this fully, we will come to realize that we are better off working together if we want to achieve our individual objectives.

6

FEEDBACK

In 2011 the UK's Chief Medical Officer, Professor Dame Sally Davies, made a startling claim that generated headlines around the world. We are losing the war against infections as a result of growing antimicrobial resistance, she said, claiming that the threat was so grave it should be included alongside terrorism, civil emergencies and cyber-attacks on the UK's national security risk register.[1] Antimicrobial resistance occurs when microorganisms, such as bacteria, change in ways that render the medications used to cure infections ineffective. Professor Davies explained that in the last fifty years, we've developed vaccines and drugs that have kept these infections largely at bay. But the picture has started to change as resistance to these medications has increased. So the next fifty years could be different if we don't start acting fast. Disease and infections that were previously easy to control will become threats to human health; standard surgical procedures and treatments, like hip replacements, chemotherapy and organ transplants, which rely on our ability to treat infections, will suddenly become much riskier. Like many complex problems, antimicrobial resistance can't be solved overnight. We will need to develop new drugs and medical procedures, and these will take years to develop. But antimicrobial resistance isn't just about the drugs. It's about human behaviour. Whenever we fail to finish a course of prescribed treatment, or put pressure on a doctor to give us drugs we don't need, we're helping to create more resistant microorganisms.

Knowing that any solutions would need to focus as much on behaviour as medicine got the Behavioural Insights Team's director of health, Michael Hallsworth, thinking. Michael, together with teams from the Department of Health and Public Health England, wanted to know if doctors would be just as receptive as the rest of the population to being given good feedback. They started by collating the information about what GP practices across England were doing, and used this to identify practices whose prescription rate for antibiotics was in the top 20 per cent for their local area. Half of this group of over-prescribers were then sent a letter, signed by the Chief Medical Officer, with feedback about their prescription habits, together with three specific things they could immediately do to reduce the number of prescriptions they gave out. For example, doctors can give patients delayed prescriptions, which enable them to get their medication in the future, so long as their symptoms persist. Alongside these tips, the doctors were told how their performance compared with others. They were informed that 'the great majority (80 per cent) of practices in [your local area] prescribe fewer antibiotics per head than yours'. When Michael and his team compared the subsequent behaviour of those doctors who received the feedback letters to that of those who got no such letter, they were surprised by the impact. Over a six-month period, GP practices receiving the feedback letters prescribed an estimated 73,400 fewer antibiotic items than those that didn't.[2] Just think about this for a moment: no changes were made to the potency of the drugs, or the financial incentives acting upon the doctors. They weren't bombarded with calls from central government haranguing them. They were just given feedback about what they were already doing, given some practical advice about what could be done differently, and told how they compared to others. They responded by prescribing tens of thousands fewer prescriptions than before.

Feedback has long been recognized as a profoundly effective tool for changing behaviour and helping us achieve our goals and the reason for this is pretty straightforward. It is very difficult for us to progress towards a goal if we don't know how well we are doing in relation to it. But, as we will see, good feedback is more than just knowing where you currently stand. It's about understanding what actions you can take to do even better. It's also about recognizing what is possible by understanding how others are doing in relation to you. We often fail, though, to collect and use feedback systematically. So this chapter will set out a simple framework for effective feedback that should spur your or others' motivation. The three golden rules of feedback are:

- **Know where you stand in relation to your goal.** You need to be able to draw on information that shows where you are in relation to your goal.
- **Make it timely, specific, actionable and focused on effort.** Ideally, you want feedback that is personal to you, clear about what you need to keep doing or do differently and given as close to event as possible.

- **Compare your performance with others.** If you can, you should also find out how well you are doing in comparison with others. In some situations, this can be the most powerful feedback of all.

Rule 1: Know where you stand in relation to your goal

If you've ever played the childhood game 'hot or cold', you'll know all about how useful feedback can be. In the game, a treasure is hidden somewhere and your task is to find it – the only information you have is whether you're getting closer or further away from the prize: 'You're cold, still cold, colder, getting warmer, warmer, warmer, very warm, hot, VERY HOT!' Eventually, you're so hot that you find the treasure. And you find it because you're continually being guided by another individual who is letting you know where you stand in relation to the ultimate objective.

In adult life, there are some situations that resemble the kind of feedback you receive when you're playing hot or cold. Think about the first time you learnt to drive a car. If it was anything like most people's experiences, it would have been a very stop/start experience. Putting your foot on the accelerator is, at first, a terrifying experience. You probably pushed too hard and over-revved the engine ('cold'), or didn't push hard enough ('colder'), before starting to get the balance right ('getting hotter'). When you pressed on the brakes for the first time, you probably caused the vehicle to jerk to a halt ('cold'). But over time, you started to learn the right level of pressure ('warmer'), and how much you needed to turn the wheel in order to turn a corner smoothly ('hot'). All of this was helped by the fact that, every time you used the brakes, pedals and wheel, you got an instant response. The car moved (or didn't) in the direction you desired (or not). This feedback enabled you to learn how to apply pressure in the right way to give you the result you wanted. This illustrates an important principle about good feedback – feedback isn't just information. It's about knowing where things are in relation to where they should be.

Lots of studies have shown just how effective feedback, focused on where you are in relation to where you should be, can be. Evidence from consumer markets shows that feedback from other purchasers (in the style of TripAdvisor, eBay and Yelp) can transform marketplaces and drive business to the best-value or highest-quality providers. An extra star on Yelp's 5-star customer rating scale, for example, increases a restaurant's revenue by 5 to 9 per cent in the following year.[3] Research on individuals striving to achieve a personal goal shows similarly powerful effects. Some of the earliest of these studies were conducted by Albert Bandura, one of the most renowned living psychologists. In one of our favourite examples, Bandura and his colleague Daniel Cervone took a group of students, and got them to do some strenuous activity on an exercise bike.[4] All the students were split into different groups. After they had completed the first round of exercise, some of them were set a challenging goal, but would receive no feedback along the way. Their goal was to increase their effort next time round by 40 per cent, and they received a reminder of this objective after they'd been exercising for five minutes. The second group were given feedback. Their performance was compared to how well they had done during the previous session. However, they were set no goals. Finally, the third group got both the goal (increase your effort by 40 per cent) as well as feedback along the way.[5] In other words, only this final group were given feedback that told them how they were performing in relation to the goal they were trying to achieve. And the results showed just how effective this combination was. Everyone improved their performance. But the students who received feedback that enabled them to understand where they were in relation to a clear goal more than doubled their performance over and above those who had received just goals or just feedback. In other words, information alone is not enough. Using feedback effectively involves taking information about how well you're doing, and then relating this to what it is you are trying to achieve – your goal.

The problem is that, in most areas of life, we don't get feedback of this kind. We charge ahead with our personal and work projects but don't get a chance to step back and think about the progress we're making towards the goals we set ourselves. And this is because most of the things we set out to achieve aren't set up like a driving lesson, in which you get an instant understanding of the relationship between your actions and their consequences. At the Behavioural Insights Team, we've found that feedback is often lacking in some of the areas where we might imagine it to be most important. When Elspeth Kirkman, who now heads our office in New York, looked at how social worker decisions might be improved, one thing in particular stood out. Social workers had no means of understanding what happened as a long-term consequence of their decisions. They got no feedback. So one of Elspeth's main recommendations was to introduce feedback loops that enabled social workers and local authorities to track the consequences of their decisions. This would – over time – enable them to build up a picture of which types of decisions, in which kinds of circumstances, are most likely to result in positive outcomes for children.

Social worker decision making might seem a world away from the goals you have set yourself, but the principles are the same. When you are considering your goals, you should seek out information that enables you to understand where you are in relation to where you want to get to. If you are seeking to lose weight and have followed the advice of earlier chapters, you will have set yourself a long-term goal and decided on the steps you need to take to get there. Getting feedback is as simple as understanding how much you weigh at each point along the way, so that you can see how you are progressing in relation to that goal. Or, if you are seeking to run the marathon in a certain time, and have broken your goal down into discrete steps, you will want to know as you progress how you are doing in relation to these steps. This could be how fast you are now able to run 10 km, or how good you are at undertaking the elements of your new training regime, such as the speed of your hill runs or the amount of weight you can lift in the gym. You will find that new apps and technologies will make the process of getting good feedback far simpler. The running app Strava, for example, not only enables you to track how fast your total run has been, but also breaks it down into different segments, each of which is given a separate time. This allows you to track your performance over time, and to compare how well you have done against others (see the third rule in this chapter).

Feedback doesn't just show us where we are going wrong, then; it enables us to understand better the impact and the progress we are making in relation to our ultimate goals. And as human beings, this is important. We like to *feel* that we are making progress, so it can sometimes help to set up our feedback systems in a way that maximizes this sensation. One study that illustrates this principle nicely was led by Ran Kivetz, who wanted to know what kinds of loyalty cards in cafes would encourage people to purchase more coffee. Would it be a card for which you needed to collect ten stamps to get your free coffee? Or would it be a card that required you to collect twelve stamps, the first two of which were pre-stamped 'bonuses'. Note that both the cards require you to do exactly the same thing: get ten stamps. But the second makes it feel as though you've already started making progress towards the goal of that free cup of coffee, and it was this card that significantly outperformed the other.[6]

This feeling of making progress is particularly important when the link between apparently mundane tasks you have to complete and your ultimate goal feel less direct. For example, in our work with job centres, we created a job search task list, which job seekers used to tick off once they had completed a task. We frontloaded this with a number of easier tasks at the beginning, such as filling out forms, attending meetings and registering for job updates, so that jobseekers would have a sense of progress and be more motivated to take on the more challenging tasks of completing CVs, attending job interviews and even retraining. In other words, knowing where you stand in relation to your goal is important. But there are ways of helping you feel that this goal is less distant than it might otherwise appear to be.

The lesson at the heart of this golden rule is to know where you stand in relation to your goal. Whether it's how much weight you've lost, how your marathon training is going, or where you and your team at work stand in relation to performance objectives for the year, it's very difficult for us to progress towards a goal if we don't know where we are on the path to achieving it. Once we've ascertained this, we can start turning to the question of what the best ways of giving and receiving feedback might be. This important question, which focuses on the specific details that matter most to spur our efforts, is the subject of the next section.

Rule 2: Make it timely, specific, actionable and focused on the effort

In 2003 Dan Candelaria and his fellow traffic engineers in Garden Grove, California, set out to tackle a familiar problem – drivers speeding through school zones.[7] Dan had tried a number of different approaches, from brighter speed limit signs to increasing the number of fines given out. But these enjoyed only modest success and the number of cyclists and pedestrians being hit in these zones remained stubbornly high. So they decided to try something new – to give drivers feedback about how fast they were driving as they drove past. They erected a radar sensor attached to a large digital 'Your Speed' sign that provided real-time information on each driver's speed. However, unlike traditional speed cameras and fines, this sign came with no financial or legal penalties. Dan was betting on the power of feedback, and challenging decades of accepted wisdom that there needed to be a stick to encourage people to comply. He had a hunch that by simply telling drivers how fast they were driving – information that was already available on their dashboard – they would slow down. And he was right.

In the years since the Garden Grove project began, developments in radar technology have meant that the cost of these signs has dropped steadily in price, and consequently 'Your Speed' signs have proliferated on roads across the globe.[8] Despite their ubiquity, the signs have consistently proven to reduce speeds, up to 10 per cent on average, an effect that seems to be well targeted at those speeding and which often lasts for several miles down the road. In fact, most traffic engineers and safety experts now consider these signs to be more effective at changing driving habits than deploying police officers with radar guns to issue tickets.[9] So, despite the lack of a penalty or indeed any new information, this deceptively simple, targeted piece of feedback has successfully reduced road traffic deaths around the world.

The speeding signs nicely illustrate three of the core principles of good feedback. It's no good telling someone that they're a bad driver, five months after their Californian speeding session. It's much better to be able to give them feedback as close to the event as possible, so that they can react to it quickly. The signs do this very nicely – by giving real-time information. Similarly, the signs give specific information that is personal to each driver. They don't average out the speed of cars in the area, or tell you that you are generally going too fast. If you're speeding, they tell you by how much. This relates to the third, and possibly the most important lesson in good feedback; it needs to be actionable. The clear message of the signs is to do something that you can actually act upon in the moment.

Good feedback, then, is all about giving people the tools to do things differently (or to keep on doing things that they are doing well). If you're thinking that this sounds all well and good for something like speeding, where you can measure what's happening very easily in real time, it's worth knowing that these same lessons are being adopted in all kinds of complex areas. The Education Endowment Foundation, for example, has identified that giving pupils timely, specific, actionable feedback is potentially one of the most important and cost-effective changes that can be made to improve children's educational outcomes.[10] At its most basic, this can mean explaining just after a pupil has performed well that 'It was good because you...' rather than simply saying 'correct'. And it should provide specific guidance on how to improve, not just telling pupils that they are wrong. In the Education Endowment Foundation's many studies of best practice in education, they have found that good feedback is one of the most effective practices one can introduce into a school. It helps pupils to progress by the equivalent of eight months of learning. This is much more effective than lots of other things that are more standard practice, like homework (equivalent progress: five months in secondary school, one month in primary) and extending the school day (two months). It's cheap too: introducing good feedback, when you factor in the training time and the costs of cover teachers , is less than £100 a pupil.

If these three principles sound obvious – that feedback should be timely, specific and actionable – then think about how infrequently they are actually acted on in the real world. Most organizations around the world still rely on giving feedback once a year during the annual performance review. But as anyone who's been through a performance review at the end of the year knows, very often the feedback is out of date by the time it's received; it's not specific enough (how can it be, when it covers an entire year of things you have done?); and that makes it harder for anyone to think about what they might do as a result. For this reason, companies around the world are abandoning the traditional way of conducting year-end performance reviews. The consulting firm Accenture, which employs over 300,000 people around the world, has recently halted annual performance reviews, and replaced them with feedback sessions that encourage shorter, sharper reflections at the end of a project.[11] At the Behavioural Insights Team we haven't abandoned end-of-year reviews altogether, but we have developed an in-house online feedback system that at the end of every project encourages everyone to give timely feedback to those they've been working with, the focus being on what people should continue doing (or could do differently).

There is one other strand of behavioural science research that holds lessons for how to give and receive good feedback. To understand it, we have to go back to the classroom with two researchers, Claudia Mueller and Carol Dweck, who were then based at Columbia University. They noticed that it seemed to be received wisdom that, if someone does a good job in the classroom, on the sports field or in any other walk of life, the right thing to do is to praise that person for their innate intelligence or their abilities. If a child gets a high score in a test or draws an especially good picture, for example, telling them how clever they are seems like the most natural thing in the world. But Mueller and Dweck were worried that praising someone for their raw intelligence might have some negative side effects. If you were led to believe that you had an innate talent for maths, what happens if you flunk your next test? Might not that make you question your abilities and would it not result in you failing to challenge yourself to undertake tasks that might risk exposing your deficiencies?

Dweck and Mueller were worried, and so they set about finding answers to some of these questions. They conducted rather than 'problems that I'm pretty good at, so I can show I'm clever'. It seemed that children praised for their intelligence appeared to learn that their performance reflected their abilities, so they attributed their subsequent poor performance to a low ability. Whereas those praised for hard work didn't ascribe their performance to their raw abilities in the same way. They responded by working harder at the subsequent task, because they had come to learn that hard graft is the way to succeed.[13]

Since these original, groundbreaking studies, Dweck has gone on to look at the application of this same set of principles to lots of different areas, almost all of which can be used to help us achieve our goals. She explains the principle by describing two different kinds of 'mindsets'. One is the 'fixed mindset', which is a belief that our qualities are set in stone, and results in us continually needing to prove ourselves over and over. When the children in the original studies were praised for their raw intelligence, they were being encouraged to think with a fixed mindset. The other mindset, encouraged in those who were given praise based on their effort, is the 'growth mindset', and it is founded on the belief that your basic qualities are things you can cultivate through your efforts.[14] Dweck's enlightening observation is that, although people do obviously differ in their abilities, 'everyone can change and grow through application and experience'. If you can give praise for effort and persistence, rather than simply for innate talent, you're more likely to be able to help yourself – and anyone you're working with – to reach their goals.

So it seems that good feedback isn't just about knowing where you stand in relation to your goal. We've seen that *when* the feedback given is important; the closer to the event the better. We've also seen that feedback that is specific and actionable is critical – you need to be able to do something as a result of the feedback (even if this is to keep doing what you're already doing). And finally, it's clear that simply praising people for being inherently good at something isn't as effective as encouraging effort and persistence with a task.

Rule 3: Compare your performance to others

We saw in Chapter 2 how planning prompts can be used to increase voter turnout. Given that relatively small shifts in voter turnout can effect the outcome of an election, it is not surprising that this has been the subject of significant research and that other tools have also proved effective – most notably comparative feedback before and after election day.

One study in particular took place back in August 2006 and focused on some 180,000 households, grouped by their location, in the run-up to the primary elections in the state of Michigan, USA.[15] Elections are good sources of experimental evidence in the US because voter records (whether someone votes, not who they vote for) are made public, which makes it easy to see what happens when you do something – like writing to would-be voters using increasingly strong forms of social pressure. In the study, some of the letters urged voters to get to the polls out of civic duty. These letters included the words 'DO YOUR CIVIC DUTY – VOTE!' The next group had the social pressure ratcheted up. In these letters, the voting records of members of the household were listed. If the person had voted in the 2004 primary and general election, the word 'voted' appeared next to their name. It was blank if they hadn't. If that wasn't enough, the letter promised the recipients that the list would be updated and sent round again *after* the election. Now, you might think this was more than sufficient mischievous activity for one band of researchers. But they decided to raise the stakes still further in the final group's letters. As for the previous group, they listed the voting records of everyone in the household. But they also listed the voting records of their neighbours. This group too were told that the tables would be updated after the election. Members of the household, in other words, would know their neighbours' voting record, but their neighbours would also know theirs.[16]

The results uncovered one of the most effective ways ever devised of getting people out to vote. The researchers themselves described the results as startling. Sending someone a letter urging them to vote out of civic duty did have a small, positive effect. But this was very small by comparison with the dramatic increase occasioned by reminding households of their own voting records. In this group, turnout leapt by 16 per cent. The biggest gain of all, though, came when one's voting record was set alongside one's neighbour's. For this group, there was a remarkable increase of over 27 per cent[17] – an increase that is almost unprecedented for any kind of campaign that doesn't involve going round face to face to get people to the booths.

We care a lot about how others perceive us and how we compare to others, and we are heavily influenced by what those around us do and say. This relates to what behavioural scientists call 'social norms'. Social norms are the values, actions and expectations of a particular society or group, and they offer guides to our behaviour. Study after study has shown that making people aware of what most other people are doing

– known as 'descriptive social norms' – can help to reinforce underlying motivations.[18] There's a good reason for this. Not only are we heavily influenced by others' behaviour; we are also often unaware of what people are *really* doing, and are prone to underestimate the good behaviour of others.[19] We tend to think that people are much more likely to be avoiding tax, consuming vast amounts of fatty food and doing next to no exercise than is really the case. And this creates an opportunity: by understanding and communicating what the prevailing social norm is, we can help motivate ourselves and others.

The Behavioural Insights Team has been using this in lots of different ways to encourage people to change their behaviour. The GPs in the opening example were one such case. Doctors, not uniquely among groups of professionals, don't simply care about what they are doing independently of others. They care also about how they are regarded by their peers, and whether they are in line with the prevailing social norms.

Perhaps our most famous example of this principle in action involved encouraging people to pay their tax. Tens of thousands of late taxpayers were sent letters with variants of these descriptive social norm messages. We found that messages simply telling people that 'Nine out of ten people pay their tax on time' were very effective at getting more people to pay the tax they owed, helping them to avoid being taken to court. But we also found that the more specific was the descriptive norm, the more effective it tended to be. When we told people that 'The vast majority of people in your local area pay their tax on time', it worked even better than the more generic message. Yet even this wasn't as effective as the message which read: 'Most people with a tax debt like yours have paid by now.' These small changes to tax letters were part of a wider programme of interventions that helped to bring forward over £200 million in revenue to Her Majesty's Revenue and Customs (HMRC, the UK's tax authority) and helped spur the creation of a tax-specific Behavioural and Customer Insights Team inside HMRC, which is dedicated to continuing this programme of work.

We are not suggesting, of course, that you get someone to write you a letter comparing your performance with those of others in your local area, as you progress towards hitting your target. But the good news is that, over the last few years, there's been an explosion in the number of apps and websites that enable you to do exactly the same thing, and many of these new tools have got comparative feedback information at the heart of them, enabling you to compare how you're doing in relation to other people. One of the best examples of this is the Fitbit, which is a wearable device that measures how much exercise you've done. The Fitbit app enables you to easily compare your performance against your friends, and to create challenges in which you compete against each other. For example, when Owain was in Singapore with Sam Hanes, who heads the Behavioural Insights Team's Singaporean office, Sam challenged him to a step challenge. Over the course of the week, they'd see who could walk the highest number of steps. It was ultimately Sam who prevailed, but they both ended up walking a bit more than they would have done in the absence of the competition.

This competitive aspect of such apps got Karen Tindall from our Australia office thinking about whether comparative feedback would be just as effective at a group level as it is at individual level. So we conducted a large study with the charity Movember, in which employees of the company Lendlease were

offered subsidised Fitbits to motivate them to increase their
levels of physical activity and measure their daily step counts.
In total, fifty teams (made up of 646 individuals) were randomly
assigned to receive one of two types of feedback. The first group
got generic leaderboard information that told them which teams
were in the lead. But the second group also got team performance
information, which told them what their current rank was as a
team, how far they were from the lead team and who the most
active individuals in the team were. The more specific group
feedback, which showed how well they were doing in relation to
other teams, helped to spur on their performance and, amazingly,
had a particularly big impact on those who were previously the
least active – precisely the people who needed the most help.

You can even use this same idea at the level of an entire
organization. Imagine, for a second, that you're the head of a
big government department in the UK. It's 2010 and you're
responsible for thousands of members of staff, and under a lot
of pressure to deliver the objectives of the government of the
day. Imagine that you've got all this to worry about and then
you hear that the prime minister has just announced that all
departments are expected to cut their carbon emissions by
at least 10 per cent. How do you feel? There is a chance that, if
you're focused on reforming the health service or thinking
about the UK's foreign policy objectives, this is not going to be
at the top of your list of priorities for the next month. But now
imagine that all departments will have their energy emissions
performance ranked alongside other each other, and that the data
will be shared at the weekly meeting of heads of department in
the form of a league table. If you're at the Department for Health,
you'll suddenly be able to see if you're performing worse or better

than your colleagues. How do you now feel? What does that do to your behaviour? This was a plan we helped to put together back in 2010 and by 2011, departmental carbon emissions had plummeted across the board. Every department achieved the 10 per cent reduction and some (like the Department for Energy and Climate Change) vastly exceeded the target.

So comparative feedback seems to work well in all kinds of situations. But before we all charge off telling everyone how they are performing relative to everyone else, we should be aware of a very important caveat, which can result in it backfiring. It is easy inadvertently to reinforce a negative social norm by emphasizing the prevalence of an undesirable behaviour. In their well-intentioned desire to highlight important issues, authorities can sometimes communicate that everyone's getting up to whatever it is that they'd prefer you didn't do. Think of signs in GP surgeries that urge you not to miss your appointment because so many other people are now failing to turn up. By signalling to people that 'everyone is doing it', you can inadvertently encourage more people to do the very thing you are trying to prevent.[20] So if you and your peers are failing to exercise more, failing to quit smoking or failing to lose weight, it's best not to invoke these kinds of 'descriptive social norms' by telling people that everyone is failing. Thankfully, there are a couple of things you can do to mitigate these effects. The first is to consider who the message is aimed at. Remember, for example, that in the doctors study, we targeted only those who prescribed the most, not those who prescribed the least. This enabled us always to be able to say that others were doing better in comparison to them. The second thing, which is especially useful for those who are already high performers, is to supplement comparative information

Feedback is an essential element towards goal achievement. But as we've seen, in some of the most critical areas of work and play, we fail to put in place mechanisms that enable us to see where we stand in relation to where we want to reach. With the growth of new technologies, there has never been a better moment to start thinking about how you can get good feedback. Banking and retail apps allow you to monitor and break down your expenditure in ways that would have been impossible for all but the most committed accountants in the past. Energy meters enable you to track your usage as never before. Fitness trackers allow you to monitor your exercise levels down to the exact number of steps. In the workplace, companies are devising new methods of enabling employees to be given feedback more frequently throughout the year (rather than just at the end of year in the dreaded performance appraisal). But in taking advantage of these new devices, you should remember that information alone isn't going to help you that much. First, you need to be able to understand where you are in relation to where you're heading. Second, you need to understand what it is that you can do to improve your performance next time round. This is why feedback that is specific, personal, actionable and focuses on effort over innate talent is so helpful; it allows you to understand what you can do with the information you're given. Finally, we've seen that, while it's amazing to get all this information about yourself, if you're able to compare how well you're doing in relation to other people, you'll probably achieve your goal even more quickly.

7

STICK

The Northern Beaches area of Sydney is an idyllic part of the world. Golden sands stretch for miles alongside national parks teeming with wildlife. The Pacific Ocean is on one side, beautiful bays looking into the city of Sydney on the other, making it possible to go for a swim or a surf in the morning before hopping on the ferry to work. But while this vision is a reality for many, for some of its residents it is a distant dream. Or at least that's how it felt for Brad, who dropped out of school when he was sixteen and ended up in a series of jobs that paid the bills for a while but offered nothing in the way of long-term prospects. He spent two years moving through a series of short-term jobs. He worked in a DVD store, spent time as an assistant in a surf shop and had a series of bar and waiting jobs in the cafes and restaurants that line the most popular beachfronts.

It was waiting tables that lit something of a fire in Brad. He became interested in the food he was serving to customers; the flavour of the dishes, the aromas they gave off. He became especially interested in meat – in the grilled steaks, the cuts of lamb and pork chops he'd regularly serve up to satisfied customers. So, by the time he was eighteen, he decided that his next role wasn't going to be another short-term job. He was going to pursue his passion, even if it meant starting again and taking a cut in wages.

The trouble for Brad was that he had no idea where to start. Then, after several weeks of soul-searching, he noticed a sign in a local butcher's shop advertising for a new apprentice. Glen, the owner of the shop, was at his wits' end after the last two apprentices had walked away only a few months into the four-year programme. This time, Glen had resolved, he was going to do things differently, so when Brad asked about the opening, Glen decided to conduct the opposite of a hard sell. He lay bare what being a butcher's apprentice was going to be like. There would be early mornings, long hours and days and days of menial tasks – chopping up endless cuts of the cheapest meats, and lots of sweeping and cleaning. To cap it all, after four years he'd still be bottom of the butchers' hierarchy. Glen believed that many young people like Brad had unrealistic expectations about what their apprenticeship was likely to entail, which helps to explain why 40 per cent of apprentices do not complete their course, and almost half of these drop-outs occur in the first year of the four-year apprenticeship.

Glen wanted to make it clear to Brad, then, that it was going to be a hard graft from day one. However, once he realized that Brad was serious, and had begun to recognize his genuine passion for meat, Glen's tone began to change. He explained that the hours spent practising his meat cuts would stand him in good stead in the long term, and that he would be able to move slowly up from the lower-quality meats to the prime steaks. Glen also emphasized that, if Brad stuck at it and gave it his all, he would teach him everything that he knew and would help him to become a qualified butcher. He would give him time and space to develop his skills, to reflect on what he was learning and to think about the areas that he was most interested in learning even more about. Glen's words had a strange effect on Brad. The years spent moving from one dead-end job to another had enabled him to understand better why it was worth putting in the hours for something that you have a passion for. So when Glen offered Brad the apprenticeship, he was determined to make it work.

Brad set himself a long-term, stretching goal, well aware that it was going to be tough. Over the years he spent hour after hour honing his skills, by chopping meat, preparing sausages and joints, and cleaning floors and fridges. But he found that the focused and effortful practice began to pay off, and he felt all the better for it. With time, Glen gave him space to try new things and even to test his own ideas and recipes in the area he enjoyed the most, which was preparing the shop's cured meats.

When Brad spoke to Rory and Edwina from the New South Wales government's own Behavioural Insights Unit, he explained that it felt as though all the hard graft was starting to pay off, and that this had encouraged him to set his sights even higher than they had been before. The lessons to Brad seemed clear. If you want to stick at a long-term goal, you have to be prepared to put in the hours; to undertake effortful practice; and to be prepared to learn from your successes and failures along the way.

The previous chapters have all focused on the tools and techniques we can put in place to help achieve our goals. This chapter is a bit different. It is about how we can make sure that we draw on these tools to help us stay with a long-term goal, particularly one that requires us to keep learning over time. The three golden rules to sticking at a goal are:

- **Practice with focus and effort.** If your goal requires you to improve your performance over time, you should remember that the quality of practice is as important as the amount of time you spend doing it.
- **Test and learn.** Once you've broken your goal down into discrete steps, you can improve your performance through experimentation – by testing the small changes, to see what works and what doesn't.
- **Reflect and celebrate success.** Take some time to reflect on what has worked well (and not so well), and make sure you celebrate what you have achieved before moving on to the next goal.

Rule 1: Practice with focus and effort

It is the final of the 2006 National Spelling Bee in America. Almost three hundred competitors, each of them a champion speller in their own right, has been eliminated after round-upon-round of increasingly difficult words. The pressure on the last couple of young contestants to perform in the contest, which is broadcast live on primetime American television, was immense. Up steps Finola Hackett, a fourteen-year-old Canadian who is asked to spell the word *weltschmerz*, a term used to describe a kind of depression brought about by comparing the world as it really is with an ideal state. So it was perhaps somewhat ironic that, after nineteen rounds of flawless spelling, it was this one that let Finola down. Up steps Katharine Close, a thirteen-year-old from New Jersey, who is trying to win the Spelling Bee at her fifth attempt. She is given the word *Ursprache*, meaning a hypothetical 'parent' language – and spells it correctly. Katharine is understandably delighted and steps up to collect her enormous, golden trophy and to be interviewed in a manner more befitting of a superstar footballer than a teenage wordsmith. 'I couldn't believe it,' she said. 'I knew [that] I knew how to spell the word and I was just in shock.' Many of the people watching the Spelling Bee that evening were also in shock at the abilities of these young people, who seemed capable of spelling words that most people twice or three times their age had not even heard of. Most of us would be forgiven for coming to the conclusion that raw, superhuman talent was behind Katharine's victory. She was, in other words, a born genius.

But unlike most people, behavioural scientists interested in how people do extraordinary things do not make assumptions of this kind. One person who was particularly interested in Katharine's victory was Angela Duckworth, a professor of psychology from the University of Pennsylvania. Duckworth was an appropriate person to be asking this question. She famously describes being told by her father during her childhood that she was 'no genius', and then, years later, of having the pleasant irony of being awarded a MacArthur Fellowship, also known as the 'Genius Grant', because it takes the form of a $625,000 no-strings-attached stipend paid to its recipients. Duckworth has spent her life trying to understand what drives success and goal achievement, and concludes that though talent does exist, it will only get you so far. What often sets apart normal people from those who go on to achieve great things is a special blend of passion and perseverance that she calls 'grit'. Might this, she wondered, also help to explain the success of Katharine and her Spelling Bee peers? So she and a group of colleagues set out to find out what the qualities of those who succeeded in the Spelling Bee might be by making contact with all of the finalists, before the final round took place. She wanted to know how much they practised, whether those who practised more were also more successful, and whether the kind of practice that they did made any difference.

The results of these kind of studies help to challenge beliefs that some people just have raw, innate gifts for a sport, musical instrument or ability to spell words. What Angela and her colleagues found, perhaps unsurprisingly, is that the kids who practised more, went further in the competition. Angela already knew that this was likely to be the case. So her second question interested her more. She wanted to know whether the *kind* of practice the kids were undertaking helped to explain their success. The researchers had identified three broad categories of practice into which most of the learning undertaken by the kids could be categorized. The first category of practice was verbal leisure activities, like reading for pleasure or playing word games. The second was being quizzed by another person or a computer. And the third was the solitary study of word spellings and their origins. This third category was what interested Angela and her colleagues the most, because it met the definition of 'deliberate practice', which has been described as a regime of effortful activities designed to improve performance.[1] Perhaps unsurprisingly, the Spelling Bee finalists identified deliberate practice as the least enjoyable, most effortful activity that they had undertaken, in contrast to the verbal leisure activities, which were considered to be fun and much less effortful.

But when Angela ran the numbers, she found that those who engaged in deliberate practice were more likely to progress in the competition. In turn, it was those children who were most prepared to persevere with the less enjoyable, but more successful, spelling strategies, that were more likely to win.

In other words, if raw talent doesn't guarantee success, neither does mindless practice. It is the quality, as well as the quantity of practice that matters (plus a bit of luck and the support of those around you). The reason it is important to make this point is that this view clashes with a hypothesis that was popularized in books like Malcolm Gladwell's *Outliers*. Such works typically examined a number of extreme examples of over-achievers and came to the conclusion that mastery of more or less any field was possible with 10,000 hours of practice. Gladwell took the argument from a (then) little-known paper, published in 1993 by Anders Ericsson (who collaborated with Angela Duckworth on her study), who had been studying violin students at the West Berlin Academy of Music and had discovered that the most accomplished of these students had put in an average of 10,000 hours of practice by the time they were twenty years old – significantly more than their peers. But this is where the argument starts to break down. Gladwell extrapolated this finding to almost every other field. The Beatles put in 10,000 hours of practice while playing the clubs of Hamburg in their early careers. Bill Gates spent approximately 10,000 hours honing his computer-programming skills before setting up one of the world's most profitable companies.

The problem with the argument was that, as Anders Ericsson would later point out, it didn't add up. For starters, the violin students, even after they had averaged 10,000 hours, were still only students. They had many years of practice ahead of them.

It was also an average figure – so lots of the students had done well in excess of 10,000 hours, while others were far below that figure. And this isn't even getting into the debate around whether more or less practice is required to master different fields. It is estimated, for example, that most international piano competitions are won by people who are over thirty years old, by which time most competitors will have racked up between 20,000 and 25,000 hours of solid practice. But Ericsson's main bone of contention was not focused on how best to calculate averages. It was that Gladwell had focused primarily on the quantity, rather than the quality of the practice.[2] Ericsson's research focuses in particular on 'deliberate practice' that requires significant amounts of focused effort, the planning of specific activities, and the receipt of feedback along the way, which enables you to push yourself to the edge of your limits to the point where you are learning most.

This book isn't about outliers. It is about how all of us can achieve our more everyday goals through a series of small changes. And most of us can probably think of something that we have done for a long period of our lives and which – at some point – we just stopped getting any better at it because we failed to stretch ourselves through deliberate practice. For example, Rory has played football for many years, and when he was at school and university he was considered to be a fairly decent player. Over the years, he estimates he might have spent between 4,000 and 5,000 hours either playing or training. But he is sadly resigned to the fact that he is not on his way to lifting the World Cup. This is because, while he has shown up to hundreds of training sessions at school, university and with his work teams, these have typically focused on some light fitness exercises, a few basic drills and then a practice game. Except in the early years, when he was still finding his feet, Rory never subsequently felt as though he was stretching himself and he was never forced to focus intently on those aspects of his game that needed the most attention – like his inability to pass or shoot accurately with his left foot, or his second-rate close control. Similarly, Owain estimates he has played around 2,000 to 3,000 hours of guitar to date and, in his late teens, became a moderately accomplished classical guitar player, driven largely by his weekly lessons. These forced him to hone skills through an approach that resembled deliberate practice. For example, he'd force himself to learn how to do a 'tremolo', which requires you to play a note repeatedly with your three plucking fingers at such high speed that you cannot pick out the single notes. It's really tough at first, but if you spend time by yourself in between lessons practising, you can gradually pick up speed until you sound reasonably accomplished. But like Rory, Owain found that after the early years of practice, in which he felt as though he made a lot of progress, he started to play 'for pleasure', stopped having lessons and found that his playing skills plateaued. They've been regressing ever since.

So, we are all capable of improving our performance in relation to a goal. But to do so we need to recognize that it will take effort and focus over a period of time and, to really learn, we need to integrate our deliberate practice into the broader approach to thinking small. It starts with the goals you set yourself. To see improvement over time, you need to be prepared to set yourself a suitably stretching goal – one that will be a challenge to meet. This could be learning a new skill that you know will push you (a language or a new musical instrument), but it might equally mean recalibrating your expectations about what can be achieved. For example, alongside the changes we made in UK Job Centres discussed in the Introduction, we also reset expectations about what level of job-searching activities might be required (from three job searches a week, which was the previous minimum, to a stretch goal of over fifty searches per week). When you then start thinking about how you can break that goal down into its constituent parts, that's the point at which you can think about the quality of the practice you undertake. For Spelling Bee champions, this might be a new category of words. For football players and musicians, it might be focusing on a specific skill. At work, it might be focusing on your ability to tell compelling narratives in presentations. In our Job Centre work, it meant focusing on the specific things that the individual job searchers could improve – for some it was maths and English skills, for others how to write an appropriate CV. And finally, none of these focused, effortful activities will get you very far if you don't have a good feedback mechanism in place to enable you to learn from the practice that you're undertaking. Are your football skills getting better? Can you spell new words? Are your presentation skills improving? Are you getting more invites to interviews?

While it is impossible for most of us to become Olympic champions, chess grandmasters, world-class spellers or master storytellers, it is possible for all of us to become better parents, managers, football players or musicians, for example. To improve our performance in relation to a long-term goal we need to set ourselves more stretching goals and then apply ourselves in a more focused way to the elements of that goal that will help us improve our performance over time. As with the rest of the insights in this book, it is the small changes you make that will add up to something bigger. But in this case, small doesn't mean easy. It requires focus, dedication and effort that, over time, will start to pay off.

Rule 2: Test and learn

Every year around a million people join the NHS organ donor register. This might seem like a lot of people, but despite the huge numbers of registrants, each day three people die in the UK because there aren't enough organs available. It was this knowledge that led the National Health Service to get in touch with the Behavioural Insights Team, to see if we could come up with any ideas that might encourage more people to join the organ donor register. Hugo Harper and Felicity Algate, who led the work, felt that there was one particularly ripe area in which we could test some new ideas. It was to change the way in which people are encouraged to sign up to the organ donor register when they renew their vehicle tax or register for a driving license. Millions of people use this website every year, so if we could make a small difference to the number of people who say 'yes' when they're prompted to join the register, it could have a huge impact.

The idea was deceptively simple. We would test eight different ways of encouraging people to sign up, and then see which one worked best. Whichever 'won' would become the new message. You can have a go for yourself now if you want by considering which one of these two messages you see is likely to be most effective (see the screenshots on page 168). Before you decide, a little heads up. One of these messages was the most effective of all, and helps to add around 96,000 extra people to the organ donor register every year compared with the standard message.

The other is the only message that *reduces* the number of people who sign up. Before you read on to learn if you were right, have a think about why you think the one you selected might have worked best, and why the other might have failed.

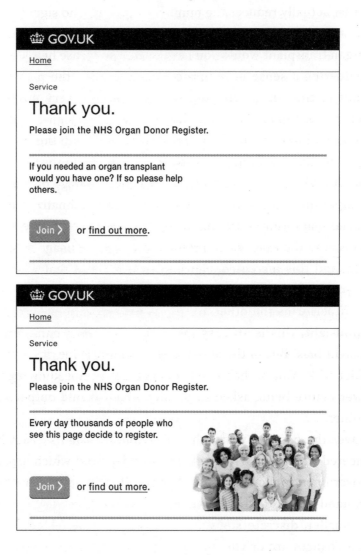

We have shown these screenshots to thousands of people over the past few years at various conferences, seminars and workshops and the majority of those we ask go for one of these two messages – either the highest performing message, or the one that actually reduces the number of people who sign up. The highest performing message is the one that reads 'If you needed an organ transplant would you have one? If so please help others.' Engendering a sense of reciprocity, in line with the principles set out in the 'Share' chapter, seems to have a very powerful effect in this context. The one that decreases the sign-ups is the message with the picture of the group of people with the message telling you that 'every day thousands of people who see this page decide to register'. It seems that the generic image of a group of people turns a serious message into a depersonalized piece of social marketing in the minds of those who see it. We know this because the exact same message *without* the image was also tested, and this *increased* sign-up rates. We find that when we tell people what the results are first and ask them to explain why one outperforms the other, it's pretty easy to generate reasons. In hindsight, this is an easy job – there's even a name for it: hindsight bias. But in the absence of this knowledge, it's a much trickier task. You probably felt this yourself – not knowing the answer before being asked to predict which would outperform the other.

Over the past six years, the Behavioural Insights Team has pioneered the use of trials to help us understand which aspects of government policy are most effective. It is an approach which goes hand-in-hand with 'chunking' – breaking down your goal into smaller, discrete steps, so that each can be tested to see which changes are driving improvements in performance. Many of these experiments are referred to throughout this book and each involves asking a simple question: does it work? If I change the first line of a letter to people who've failed to pay their tax on time by telling them how many other people have paid, will it result in more people paying on time? (Answer: yes.) If I send people a message with an infrared picture attached of their home, showing how much energy they are wasting, and compare that to the same message without the infrared image, will it get more people to insulate their homes? (Answer: no, it *decreases* the number of people who do so, possibly because the image shows a glowing home, which some might interpret as lovely and cosy.)

If you think this experimental approach is limited to niche parts of the UK government, you'd be wrong. We saw in the 'Set' chapter how these same principles have been used by the British Olympic cycling team. They have also underpinned the success of Formula 1 teams seeking to make small improvements on their opponents; they are used by the Education Endowment Foundation to find out what works in school settings; and they even explain why tech companies like Google choose particular layouts and colour schemes. Google, like lots of other internet companies, is constantly testing small changes against existing practices to see which is best, and recently found that they were able to boost advertising revenue by some $200 million by making a small change to the shade of blue they used for the Google toolbar.[3]

What each of these tests had in common was the same recognition that comes to those who try and guess which of the organ donation messages might work best: an admission that they did not know what was going to work best. And that is, in many ways, the biggest barrier for all of us to overcome. As the

Freakonomics authors Stephen Dubner and Steven Levitt have argued, the hardest three words in the English language are not 'I am sorry' or 'I love you'; they are: 'I don't know.'[4] The problem is that, in almost all areas of work, life and play, we fail to accept that we don't really know what works and what doesn't. As the chief executive of the Behavioural Insights Team, David Halpern, has argued, it is the dirty secret of governments around the world that we do not know conclusively whether we are doing the right thing or not; whether a programme we have invested huge amounts of resources in – a new curriculum, employment support package, judicial sentence or so forth – is actually working.

It is only when we go and trial these programmes in a way that enables us to see what would have happened if we did nothing (by testing the new intervention against a control), that we can be certain that the programme is having the effect we expected it to have.[5] The best illustrations of this are in those unfortunate instances where trials show that a programme we assumed was having a positive impact was actually having very little impact, or indeed a negative one. One such programme was called Scared Straight. It was developed in the US to deter young people from falling into a life of crime. The idea was simple. The kids would typically visit an adult prison, where they would hear about the reality of prison life from the inmates themselves.[6] It might also include living the life of a prisoner for the day or receiving a deliberatively aggressive presentation by prisoners.[7] Scared Straight was picked across the USA and copied by other justice systems around the world. Some early evaluations seemed to show that the programme was achieving great results and there was even a documentary made about the programme in 1978, which went on to win the Academy Award for Best Documentary

Feature. The trouble was, the programme didn't work. In fact, it was worse than that. A major evaluation of nine Scared Straight programmes found that they actually increased crime rates among those who'd made the prison visits. By 1997 a report to the US Congress, which reviewed 500 crime prevention evaluations, placed it on the 'what does not work' category. That's why it's so important to test new ideas before you introduce them at scale.

Now, we know that it's not going to be possible for you to run hundreds of evaluations of different ways of becoming a better manager, losing weight, quitting smoking, improving your musical skills or learning a foreign language. But it does require you to admit to yourself that you do not always know what works best, demonstrating that it is worth trying out a variety of approaches to help you see which actions are best for helping you to achieve your desired outcomes. Following the framework set out in this book will make it easier to build this experimental approach into the way you set about achieving your goal. By breaking your goal down into a set of manageable steps and seeking feedback against a set of alternative approaches, you can start to identify the small changes you can make that add up to something bigger. For example, if your goal is to burn more calories every day for the next six months, you can try walking to work some days and seeing if that is more effective than getting the bus but always using the stairs to get to your sixth-floor office. On other days, you can do both. By using a Fitbit device or smart phone, you can monitor which of the two is most effective by measuring calories burned, and you can also judge which you are most able to build into your daily routine. If you are trying to save money, you can test a variety of different approaches and then monitor which of these results in you setting most aside. Some months you can try transferring money from your account into an account that cannot be raided (similar to the commitment account we saw in the 'Commit' chapter). During other months you can try setting aside a specified amount every time you don't buy something that you would ordinarily have bought (that latte on the way to work). After several months, you can see which seems to be accumulating the most cash and then test variations of that particular method to see if you can improve it even more. Or as a new parent, you may want to experiment with different routines, times or methods for helping put your child to bed. The experimental approach can also be used to test some of your long-held assumptions in a fun way. When one of our colleagues declared that he thought organic carrots were vastly superior to ordinary carrots, Owain put it to the test with a blind taste challenge. No one could tell the difference. Over the years they subsequently tested orange juices (expensive = superior); wine (cheap is sometimes better) and even gin and tonic (some in-depth research in this area led us to believe the tonic drives the taste more than the gin!).

By testing and learning, we hope that you are able to adopt an approach which accepts you are not going to get it right first time, every time. But if you truly embrace the experimental method, you should see each of those failures as a little extra information that makes it more likely you will ultimately achieve your goal. That's because you'll have identified the things that you now know don't work – like the Scared Straight programme – and you should therefore stop doing. Along the way you will no doubt also start identifying those things that seem to work best for you.

Rule 3: Reflect and celebrate success

Imagine that you are an undergraduate student. Alongside your studies, you have a couple of jobs to help pay for your text-books and the occasional night out. For one of your jobs, you are a paid fundraiser for your university, which involves calling former alumni to persuade them to part with their cash. The former students are from across the academic spectrum – from music to business – and include people who have donated before, as well as those who haven't. So you know that some calls are likely to be successful, while others will require a bit more effort. One day you are about to start a shift, when you are asked to gather round to hear a short talk from a graduate student of the university's anthropology department. You listen intently as she explains the difference the money raised by you and your fellow fundraisers has made to her life. It was as a result of the calls made by you all, she explains, that she was able to travel and collect data for her research. And this research is helping to add to the body of knowledge of anthropology. You ask her questions about her research – where she travelled to, what it was focused on – and you are interested in how she used the money to support her endeavours. Money that you had helped raise. In total, the graduate student's talk lasts only fifteen minutes, but you remember feeling a rush of warmth about it afterwards, as you pick up the phone for the thousandth time to see if you can collect more donations from alumni to the university's coffers.

By now, you won't be surprised to learn that this scene was part of an experiment, conducted by a friend of the Behavioural Insights Team, Adam Grant, who we encountered in the 'Share' chapter in relation to his work on people helping one another to succeed.[8] Grant, then at the University of North Carolina at Chapel Hill, was interested in the fact that those working in public service – whether as a doctor, social worker or police officer – are not solely motivated by money, but also by the potential to make a difference to the communities that they serve. But Grant also realized that public service workers often never get to see the longer-term impact of their work. So his study was therefore designed to see what would happen to students' fundraising efforts when they got a chance to reflect upon what they had helped to achieve by hearing a motivational talk from a graduate student who'd received funding as a result of their activities.

Grant created two groups of students. One group received the talk from the graduate student, the other group got nothing extra and went about their business as usual. Grant then measured how many financial pledges each person in each group collected on average in the month after the talk had taken place. The students who heard the talk showed a dramatic increase in the number of donations and amount pledged (more than double). By contrast, there was only a modest (and statistically insignificant) increase in the number of pledges and amount of money donated in the group who had not heard the talk. It seemed that being able to see and understand the positive benefits of the work that the fundraisers had been involved in provided a big boost in motivation for those undertaking what can sometimes feel like a challenging task.

We can all do more to reflect on the impact of the things we try to achieve in our work and our personal lives. It's just that we do not routinely create opportunities to do so. As Grant's study nicely shows, it helps to remind people about the true impact of their work on real people's lives. You just need to think imaginatively about how you might go about doing this. For example, Elaine, Rory's wife, is a palliative care doctor and one of the things she finds most rewarding about her job is when a family of the patient she has looked after writes her a thank you note. The problem across the health system generally is that by the time patients and families have returned from hospital, they lose touch with those who have helped them and cannot always find a way to engage with them further down the line. This was exactly what Owain and his wife Sophie experienced a couple of months after getting back from hospital following the birth of their first son. They wanted to send a card to the specific people who had supported them, but realized that they had no names of the individuals or means of contacting them directly beyond hanging out in the hospital wards. Very often all that is required in these instances is a simple mechanism that facilitates contact. A very nice example of how this can be done is to be found at a hospital in Sydney, Australia, which makes a point of writing to patients to ask *them* how they are getting on a month after they have left hospital. It provides a simple mechanism through which the patients are – usually – able to thank the staff, and to reflect on the care that they have received.

The idea of reflecting on success is a mantra that the Behavioural Insights Team has taken up in a number of different ways. For example, we have run interventions with school pupils to test different ways of encouraging them to go to university and found that just providing pupils or their parents with information – for example about the long-term benefits of attending university – are not effective. What does seem to work is pupils hearing about what it's like to go to university from former pupils;

such pupils inevitably dwelt on the lifestyle benefits as well as future career prospects. Similarly, at the Behavioural Insights Team's start-the-week meeting, we always set aside time for what we call 'Whoops of the Week'. These are opportunities for anyone to highlight something positive that someone *else* has done that helped them out or was particularly impressive. It's a nice way of saying thanks to someone else, but also provides an opportunity for the whole team to reflect on the things that their colleagues have done that have really made a difference – often to the lives of others, rather than just their own. We want to encourage you to do the same by reflecting upon what you have achieved once you've reached your goal, especially if you've had an impact upon other people's lives in getting there.

Of course, it is likely that some of the goals you set yourself will be too personal (climbing a mountain, losing some weight, or finding a new job) to impact significantly upon others. In these instances we would encourage you to take a slightly different strategy: take time out for reflection about what you have learnt along the way. You can do this during the period you spend achieving your goal, and after you have been successful (or not). This is a strand of research being pursued by another friend of the Behavioural Insights Team, Harvard researcher Francesca Gino and her colleagues, who have conducted a number of studies that explicitly encourage people to reflect on what they have learnt before rushing into the next set of challenges.[9] The common finding in this research is that spending a small amount of time to reflect on what you have learnt pays dividends in the long term.

Gino shows this in numerous settings, including in a study conducted in the call centre of a global IT, consulting and outsourcing company based in India. The study focused on employees during their initial weeks of training. All the call centre trainees went through the same technical training, but with one crucial difference. One group spent the last fifteen minutes of each day reflecting on and writing about the lessons they had learnt that day, while the other group just kept working for another fifteen minutes. At the final training test at the end of one month, the trainees who reflected on a daily basis for fifteen minutes performed more than 20 per cent better, on average, than those in the control group. Francesca's argument is that this kind of reflection is not a replacement for the kind of deliberate practice that we discussed earlier in this chapter. Far from it. Rather, it should be seen as a powerful complement to it. The researchers give the example of a cardiac surgeon engaged in effortful practice under the guidance of an instructor. Her aim is to become better at performing surgery as quickly as possible. But there is a limit to how much better she will become through practice alone. Setting aside a small amount of time to reflect on progress alongside the experiential learning will help her to improve more quickly. And you should do the same as you progress, or as you suffer setbacks along the way to achieving your goal. You should think about what you have learnt along the way, and use this to inform what you might try (and test) next. When you have ultimately achieved your goal, it would be beneficial to spend some time reflecting on your achievements before moving on to the next objective.

Before you reach your goal, however, we want you to think about putting in place one further small change that we think will ensure you look back on your achievements with pride and will help you to move on to even greater things in the future; think of ways of celebrating and capturing the moment when you ultimately achieve your objective. This isn't just a nice thing to do; there's also a good psychological reason for doing it, especially if your goal has been tough to achieve and has required you to endure suffering along the way. It relates to a little-known psychological construct known as the 'peak-end rule', in which we judge our experiences based on how they felt at their end and at their most intense points, rather than (as we might imagine) on the sum of pleasure or pain that the experience gave us.

Think about going to the dentist, for example. You might think that it would be better to get your teeth drilled as quickly as possible. But the research suggests that what is more important than the duration is how painful the worst moments were, and how the experience felt at the end. In one of the original studies to document the effect,[10] Daniel Kahneman and his colleagues subjected trial participants to two very similar, unpleasant experiences, which Kahneman later described as a 'mild form of torture'.[11] The first involved having one hand immersed in cold water at 14°C for thirty seconds. The temperature was designed to be moderately painful, but not excruciatingly so, for the participants. If it sounds too warm to be painful, try it for yourself and see! Seven minutes later, they were subject to a second bout of mild torture. This time their other hand was kept in the water at 14°C for thirty seconds. But after the thirty seconds had elapsed, they had to keep their hand in for another thirty seconds while the temperature was very gradually raised to 15°C (still painful but surprisingly less so than a degree colder).[12] When the participants were asked which they wanted to repeat, a significant majority chose the longer trial, implying that they preferred more pain overall. The experiment was designed to create a 'conflict between the interests of the experiencing and the remembering selves'. The experience was clearly worse in the second form of torture. But experience and memory are different things and what Kahneman and his colleagues found was that our evaluations of experiences are dominated by the pleasures and discomforts we feel at the worst and final moments (hence the peak-end rule).

This means that when we are designing services, or the way we go about achieving our goals, we should think about how we can dampen the moments of unpleasantness; maximize the peaks of pleasure; and make sure that those final moments when we're about to achieve our ultimate objective are as pleasurable as possible. Ensure, then, that you make the time to celebrate those final moments – by enjoying a glass of brandy at the top of the mountain or celebrating with your team after meeting your annual targets. Better still, try and capture that particular moment in some way, for example with a photograph of yourself crossing the finishing line or celebrating with your children on exam results day. It will help you to remember why you went through the months of effort to get there, as well as make you more resilient for your next challenge.

When we set out to achieve a goal, particularly a long-term goal that requires us to learn a new skill over time, it's easy for us to charge ahead and to keep doing the same thing time and again. If we do so we will find that, even when we think we are practising, we won't really be learning, we'll be going through the motions. If we want to get better at a task over time, we need to think about how we are going to learn, so the best place to start is by thinking about how you are going to practise – by breaking your goal down and engaging yourself in effortful practice focused on making incremental improvements to how you go about tackling the task. If you do this, you'll find that testing and trialling new ideas and new techniques will start to come naturally. You might not be able to conduct a large-scale randomized evaluation, but you will be able to learn from the feedback you get along the way, and by trying out small changes one at a time to see what effect they have on what you are trying to achieve. Finally, once you start making progress, or even if you have a few setbacks along the way, you need to set some time aside for yourself to reflect on what seems to be working and what is holding you back. If you can do all of these things, you'll be able to start thinking about how you will celebrate when you finally achieve your goal. Then, of course, with a bit more reflection, you'll be able to start thinking about what you might want to focus on next.

CONCLUSION

We are often encouraged to think big because it implies that we want to achieve great things. After all, if we had the choice, why wouldn't any of us go big rather than small? But we have shown that when you have an ambitious, long-term objective, you are unlikely to meet your goal if you don't get the small details right along the way. To achieve big, you need to think small.

The science

To understand why thinking small makes sense, we need to understand the science of decision making. That's why, in writing this book, we have examined hundreds of studies that look at how we go about achieving our goals. In particular, we have seen the importance of understanding the different ways in which human beings process information and take decisions. We have a slow, reflective system; and we have a fast, automatic system. The slow system enables us to learn how to drive a car. The fast system allows us to drive effortlessly once we've mastered the art.

The key to thinking small is to understand how and when to deploy the slow system, and how and where to encourage the fast system to take over. This isn't easy, because although the fast system enables us to live our lives in a complex world (for example, driving a car without having to think actively about using the pedals), it is also prone to make systematic errors. At the same time, we don't have sufficient mental 'processing power' to take all decisions using our reflective system. We have limited cognitive bandwidth, and will fail if we go beyond what our attention span can handle. That is why the small details matter. Thinking small helps us to reach big goals by using the relative strengths of the fast and slow systems, while avoiding the pitfalls of both.

One of the most important illustrations of the fast and slow systems in practice is understanding the effect of time. Our fast system has a strong preference for rewards in the present and would prefer to delay effortful decisions till tomorrow. Our slow system is capable of understanding that there might be a more virtuous set of preferences, but only if gratification is delayed until tomorrow and more challenging decisions are grappled with today. Many of the tools of a thinking small approach are aimed at helping to lock us into this more virtuous path, including by co-opting the fast thinking system as a friend and not a foe.

Thinking small, reaching big

Thinking small provides you with the scaffolding around which you can build your goal and set about achieving it. It shouldn't be thought of as a set of rigid rules, so don't worry – you won't have to apply each of the seven tools in every situation. But of course, the more supports you put in place, the stronger your scaffolding is likely to be.

Like any structure, you begin with the foundations. It starts with how you go about setting your goal in the first place. This was where we began to encourage you to engage, at a deep level, your reflective system. We encouraged you to spend time thinking about what you want to achieve in the first place, drawing on the evidence from the wellbeing research to help you focus on improving your life at work, rest and play. And we showed that breaking your goal down into manageable steps will help you to reach your ultimate objective faster. We then set out how to set yourself up for success by planning how to achieve your goal. In particular, we highlighted how you can use 'if-then' plans that cognitively link actions to specific moments in our daily routine. By repeating these actions in response to the same cues, we can start to develop habits that automate actions that might previously have been effortful and challenging. You will slowly find your fast system taking over.

We then set out the tools that will help further strengthen your scaffolding by keeping you motivated along the way. In helping you commit to achieve your goal, we wanted you to understand how you could overcome the tensions all of us encounter between our present and our future selves. By making a written, public commitment to a future goal, we are much more likely to follow through on our intentions. Next we highlighted that reward systems can be very effective, but they can also backfire if – yes, you've guessed it – you don't get the small details right.

We also saw how most people seem to think of achieving goals as a personal betterment project. But that working with others not only makes achieving your goal more enjoyable, it also increases the chances of getting there. We also highlighted how vital good feedback is – because it's hard to achieve anything if you don't know how well you are doing along the way. In addition, we examined the ties that hold your scaffolding together. We saw that you need to undertake deep practice in order to really hone your skills and to experiment to find out what works best for your specific goal. And lastly, we encouraged you to take the time to reflect and celebrate when you do reach your goal, not only to enjoy the fruits of your labour, but also to learn the lessons that can help spur you on in your next challenge.

Common sense and counterintuition

Despite the evidence that shows how effective this set of tools can be, we know that there will still be those who will reject our methods. We anticipate that there are likely to be two central criticisms.

The first is that small thinking is fine for small goals. But sometimes you have to make big changes if you are to achieve anything substantial, and for this you need a completely different approach. People are likely to point to the emblematic examples to make the point. If we turn our attention to the unhappy subject of war for a minute, in the aftermath of the Second World War, when Europe was on its knees, we needed a Marshall Plan (in which the USA gave $12 billion in economic support to help rebuild Europe) and not a set of little initiatives. Sometimes you need to take big, bold steps, it will be argued. Indeed, Tim Harford has recently argued that marginal gains work fine for continuous improvement (à la Sir David Brailsford and Team Sky), but huge leaps often come from more radical innovations and changes. To make a cycling comparison, he cites the Scottish racing cyclist Graeme Obree (nicknamed the Flying Scotsman), who twice broke the world hour record in the 1990s by radically changing his riding position and bike design.[1]

But the point is not that we shouldn't set our sights high or make major changes. Far from it. It is that focusing purely on the lofty, distant goal is unlikely to help us work out how to get there. The Marshall Plan had a bold vision, but also a clear plan of how to execute it. And this is a really critical point. Lots of people have amazingly ambitious, long-term goals. But few make them happen. And that's where small thinking comes into play. As we argued in the opening chapter ('Set'), it's not good enough to have a distant dream. The key is to connect that dream to the realities of daily life. So if you want to turbo boost your team's performance at work, or even turn around a failing school or hospital, it is unlikely you will achieve these goals without identifying the series of small steps necessary to get there.

In addition, we have suggested that sometimes in order to achieve your goal you need to make some changes to your daily routines, so rather than just cutting down how much alcohol you drink you should in fact set up simple but bold rules such as stopping drinking alcohol at home. Or rather than just aiming to improve your work–life balance so you can see more of your family, you should commit to not responding to any emails after 7 p.m. or work from home two days per week. Or, if you're trying to improve your school's performance, you may want to redirect your funding from teaching assistants to invest in training that helps teachers to give better feedback to their pupils.

The second likely criticism is a more subtle, and perhaps pernicious, one. It is that small thinking is nothing but common sense. It's not a huge surprise, some will argue, that breaking your long-term goal down into easy-to-manage steps will make it more likely you will achieve your goal. Nor will many people be amazed to learn that getting other people to help you achieve your goal will make achieving it more probable. Again, we agree. A lot of the lessons in *Think Small* are what we regard as applied common sense. The trouble with applied common sense, however, is that we often fail to apply it and, even when we do, we rarely do so in a consistent or disciplined way. This is something we have found time and again at the Behavioural Insights Team. Isn't it obvious, we are asked, that people are more likely to pay their tax if you write them a letter that's easy to understand (rather than a four-page letter full of complex legal language). 'Yes,' we say, 'so why is it that we continue to send out millions of letters to people every year that are full of legal language that no one understands?' Or isn't it obvious that if you agree clear deadlines, roles and responsibilities, track progress and give specific, timely feedback that you will deliver projects on time and budget? Again yes, but why do so many projects over-run? Sometimes it's difficult for us to apply the simplest of lessons and that's why we have set out *Think Small* as a straightforward framework around which we can build our goals.

We have also seen, however, that many of the *Think Small* lessons are not so obvious. Some of the most important principles at the heart of this book are counterintuitive. Remember the very first section of the 'Set' chapter? We saw how we routinely pursue goals that are unlikely to improve our wellbeing and make us happier. It seems that we do not intuitively appreciate the crucial role that relationships, health and giving have upon our wellbeing. Or how we have a tendency to try and achieve several ambitious objectives all at the same time, without realizing that doing so is setting ourselves up to fail.

In the 'Commit' chapter, we saw how just telling people what our goals are can backfire, while making specific plans public and writing them down has been shown to have a big, positive impact. We saw too how appointing a loved one to be your commitment referee is not a great strategy – better to have a trusted third party, who is prepared to follow through with the consequences of your commitment contract. We showed how much more willing others are to help than we might imagine (even complete strangers); and how incentives can crowd out our intrinsic motivations if we don't set them at a sufficiently high level, or – better – in a way that goes with the grain of our underlying objectives.

So it turns out that many of the lessons are not common sense at all. They go against many of our intuitions, which is why we have continually emphasized the importance of getting the small details right. If you do, while you may not become an Olympian or millionaire CEO overnight, you can make meaningful differences to your life and the lives of others.

Sharing and sticking

We thought long and hard about how to finish this book. In the end, though, we wanted to return to themes that have really resonated with us in writing it – which has been our joint goal over the past twelve months.

Perhaps the most important of these is the significance of other people in supporting us to achieve our goals. *Think Small* couldn't have been written without the work of everyone at the Behavioural Insights Team and the thousands of people who have helped design and implement our many hundreds of trials over the years. It would also not have been possible without the support of Elaine and Sophie, our wives, who have given us support, counsel and feedback along the way. It was also evident, of course, in our choice to co-author this book. This allowed us to share ideas, challenge each other and make the task much more enjoyable. So we wanted to reiterate one of the best bits of advice we've ever been given: be selfish by helping and working with others.

Alongside urging you to work with others, we also encourage you to push yourself by taking on some things that we know will represent more of a challenge. This takes us to the final pieces of the puzzle, which are to keep practising, ideally by focusing on the improvements you can make to the things you find most challenging; and to keep testing, by trying new techniques that enable you to discover what's working and what isn't going so well.

We did exactly that when writing this book. We challenged ourselves by grappling with new ideas from the behavioural sciences. And during the writing process, we honed our working practices, testing several different ways of writing together before finding one that worked really well.[2] The good news is that overcoming these challenges will help you to develop your own resilience and goal skills. As the great Professor James Heckman has said: 'Skills beget skills.' In other words, once you have successfully achieved one goal, you will have set up the scaffolding for achieving future goals. We certainly hope that is true for you.

APPENDIX 1 and 2

1 THINKING SMALL IN ACTION

We thought it might be useful to set out a handful of goals using our seven-step framework, so that you could use these as a template for setting out your own goals. We have chosen four common goals as examples, but you can apply the same approach to your specific goal. Of course, not every step and rule will be applicable for each goal (see appendix 2 for a full list of rules). So while in the first goal we show how every rule could be used, for the others we show how you can use a combination of selected rules. We'd like you to think of this seven-step framework as the scaffolding around which you can achieve your goals.

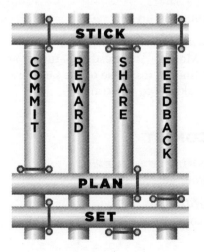

GOAL: Get fit

STEP 1: SET

☐ *Choose the right goal*
Get healthy and improve your fitness – by running a marathon

☐ *Set a specific target and deadline*
Run a marathon in under four hours by 31 May (e.g. in 5 months' time)

☐ *Break it down into manageable steps*
Set up a weekly training regime focusing on different elements (interval training; medium distance runs; longer runs; swim/cycle) and enter into a 10k (Feb), half marathon (March) and marathon (May)

STEP 2: PLAN

☐ *Keep it simple*
Train four times a week

☐ *Create an actionable plan*
Schedule training sessions in your diary for Monday (interval training) and Wednesday mornings (medium distance) before work, and on a Saturday morning (long distance runs) and Sunday morning (swim or cycle)

☐ *Turn the plan into habits*
Repeat your Monday, Wednesday, Saturday and Sunday morning routines in response to the same cues (alarm goes off, have light breakfast, go and train)

STEP 3: COMMIT

☐ *Make a binding commitment*
Commit to your goal and plan

☐ *Make it public and write it down*
Email work colleagues about your target time and training plan

☐ *Appoint a commitment referee*
Ask a work colleague to act as a referee for your weekly run targets

STEP 4: REWARD

☐ *Put something at stake for a headline objective*
Book a long weekend away with your partner for June, which you can only take if you achieve your goal

☐ *Build good habits through smaller rewards*
Only listen to you favourite podcast and albums when running

☐ *Beware of backfire effects*
Sign up to give £200 to Chelsea FC (the football team you loathe) if you finish in a time over four hours, and £500 if you do not complete or run in any marathon by May

STEP 5: SHARE

☐ *Ask for help*
Agree with your partner that on nights before training sessions you both won't drink and will go to bed before 10 p.m.

☐ *Tap into your social networks*
Find a running partner for the long distance runs on Saturdays and cycle/swim with your partner on Sundays

☐ *Join a group*
Fundraise in partnership with others (e.g. sign-up with a charity that has a big group of people signed up for the same marathon)

STEP 6: FEEDBACK

☐ *Know where you stand in relation to your goal*
Keep a run tracker to record training times and distances

☐ *Make feedback timely, specific and actionable*
During training runs and races keep track of time vs required average speed (5 mins 35 seconds per kilometre)

Compare yourself to others
Compare training plan and run trackers with others training
for a marathon

STEP 7: STICK

Practice with focus and effort
Slowly build up stamina and pace, focusing every run on
improving target times

Test and learn
Test different types of trainers, socks and strapping to reduce
foot blisters during longer runs

Reflect and celebrate
Hang a photo of yourself crossing the line in the kitchen, along
with a beneficiary of the charity you fundraised for

GOAL: Spending more time with my young kids

STEP 1: SET

☐ *Choose the right goal*
Strengthen social relationships – with your young family

☐ *Set a specific target and deadline*
Help read, bath and get your kids to sleep at least three work nights per week throughout 2017

STEP 2: PLAN

☐ *Keep it simple*
Leave work by 5 p.m. on Mondays, Tuesdays and Fridays

☐ *Create an actionable plan*
Get to work by 7.30 a.m. and schedule meetings to finish by 4.30 p.m. Set a daily reminder/alarm on your phone for 4.45 p.m. with a photo of your kids. If this reminder goes off and you're still working then shut down the computer and finish any urgent work after you've put the kids to bed

STEP 3: COMMIT

☐ *Make a binding commitment*
Make a promise to your kids on Sunday evening what you will read with them that week and email this list of books to a designated work colleague

STEP 4: REWARD

☐ *Beware of backfire effects*
When you don't meet your weekly target, you have to buy your colleague's lunches for a week and your kids choose your clothes for the weekend

STEP 5: SHARE

☐ *Ask for help*
Ask your office manager to help manage diary to reduce late meetings and overnight travel, and leave the office together at 5 p.m. on Mondays, Tuesdays and Fridays

STEP 6: FEEDBACK

☐ *Know where you stand in relation to your goal*
Keep track of progress on calendar in kitchen at home, and send a photo of this to your colleague on a weekly basis

STEP 7: STICK

☐ *Test and learn*
Try singing songs as well as reading different types of stories to your kids (picture books, lift-the-flap books, longer stories) and see what they enjoy most and what helps settle them for bed most effectively

☐ *Reflect and celebrate*
Every month ask your kids what books they liked most and share these with friends

GOAL: Be a better manager

STEP 1: SET

☐ *Choose the right goal*
Strengthen social relationships at work – by improving communication and feedback with your team

☐ *Set a specific target and deadline*
Improve team scores related to staff engagement, communication and feedback in the next annual all-staff survey

STEP 2: PLAN

☐ *Keep it simple*
Block out a dedicated period of time in your diary (9 a.m.–2 p.m. on Fridays) for catch-ups and feedback

☐ *Create an actionable plan*
Use Fridays to schedule one-to-ones with staff that you manage directly (on rotating monthly basis), hold weekly drop-in sessions for all staff to seek and provide feedback, establish a standing item at team meetings to share successes and challenges and send a monthly email to team summarizing the key priorities, achievements and lessons learnt

☐ *Turn the plan into habits*
Dedicate fifteen minutes at the end of each day to collate and analyse feedback and thirty minutes first thing on Friday mornings to prep for catch-ups and weekly feedback slots at team meetings. Encourage team to do the same by sending default calendar reminders to all team members

STEP 3: COMMIT

☐ *Make it public and write it down*
Write to your team and manager committing to weekly team meetings, drop-in sessions, feedback sessions and emails, and schedule a three-month review to assess progress

STEP 4: REWARD

 Build good habits through smaller rewards
Set up a staff reward scheme (up to £150) to recognize team members who provide the most honest and actionable feedback during team feedback sessions. Team members are encouraged to spend £100 on an experience for themselves and £50 on someone who has helped in relation to the area they've been giving feedback on

STEP 5: SHARE

Tap into your social networks
Set up a rapid feedback system, where all staff provide feedback to each other at the end of projects

Join a group
Link up with others across the organization seeking to improve communication and management, by establishing monthly peer sharing and learning sessions

STEP 6: FEEDBACK

Know where you stand in relation to your goal
Keep track of weekly emails and feedback given, and review these on a monthly basis (in between three-month reviews)

STEP 7: STICK

Test and learn
Try different ways of structuring feedback sessions and emails to see what stimulates the most productive discussions and engagement

GOAL: Make a difference

STEP 1: SET

☐ *Choose the right goal*
Give to others – by fundraising and mentoring a young person at risk through a local charity

☐ *Set a specific target and deadline*
Start a twelve-month mentoring programme by e.g. May 2017

☐ *Break it down into manageable steps*
Finalize agreement with charity by e.g. February 2017 and start mentoring and fundraising in e.g. May 2017

STEP 2: PLAN

☐ *Keep it simple*
Meet with my mentee every Tuesday at 5 p.m.

☐ *Create an actionable plan*
Schedule to leave work by 4 p.m. every Tuesday, and plan a mix of educational, fun and reflective weekly activities, as well as three challenges to complete together over the course of the year

STEP 3: COMMIT

☐ *Make it public and write it down*
Set up a fundraising webpage that includes details of commitments to meet mentee every week and undertake three challenges together to fundraise £1,000 over the year

STEP 4: REWARD

☐ *Build good habits through smaller rewards*
Treat yourself to favourite takeaways after mentoring

STEP 5: SHARE

☐ *Ask for help*
Ask family, friends and colleagues for suggestions for activities and challenges to do with your mentee

☐ *Tap into your social networks*
Use social media networks to help fundraise

STEP 6: FEEDBACK

☐ *Know where you stand in relation to your goal*
Keep a log of the activities and challenges done, plus amount fundraised vs target

☐ *Make feedback timely, specific and actionable*
Ask your mentee for regular feedback on your activities and challenges, and assess their progress. Cross-check this with others who are close to your mentee (e.g. parents, charity, school reports) for their views on progress

STEP 7: STICK

☐ *Practice with focus and effort*
Practise different mentoring and coaching techniques, in particular by using active constructive responding and developing your active listening skills

☐ *Reflect and celebrate*
At the end of twelve months, ask mentee about favourite activities and most important discussions/lessons – and create a photo for you both to keep related to these moments

2 THE GOLDEN RULES

SET
- Choose the right goal
- Focus on a single goal and set a clear target and deadline
- Break your goal down into manageable steps

PLAN
- Keep it simple
- Create an actionable plan
- Turn the plan into habits

COMMIT
- Make a commitment
- Write it down and make it public
- Appoint a commitment referee

REWARD
- Put something meaningful at stake
- Use small rewards to build good habits
- Beware of backfire effects

SHARE
- Ask for help
- Tap into your social networks
- Use group power

FEEDBACK
- Know where you stand in relation to your goal
- Make it timely, specific, actionable and focused on effort
- Compare your performance with others

STICK
- Practice with focus and effort
- Test and learn
- Reflect and celebrate success

ACKNOWLEDGEMENTS

This book would have been impossible to write without the support, advice and research findings of our amazing colleagues at the Behavioural Insights Team (BIT), or the Nudge Unit as it is more commonly known. While there are now too many people working at BIT to name everyone, we would like to give special thanks to the founding members of the team, with whom we started this ride back in 2010: David, Samuel, Simon, Felicity and Michael (Hallsworth). David is our chief executive, and continues to be the driving force and intellectual heart of BIT. He has been incredibly giving with his time and thoughts over the years and shaped our thinking and lives in ways that he, or we, will probably never fully realize. Sam and Felicity now head our offices in Singapore and Manchester, and Simon and Michael lead our programmes on home affairs, international programmes, health and tax. Their sharp thinking, wit and friendship have kept us laughing and learning along the way.

Alongside the founding team, we quickly brought in a group of people who helped to develop the BIT's expertise in new areas. So we would like to say a huge thanks to Michael (Sanders), who oversees our research and evaluation, and Elspeth, who heads our New York office; to Hugo, Jo, Alex (Gyani), Alex (Tupper), Raj, Marcos, Ed, Olly, Andy and Nicky, who were brave enough to join BIT in its early days; and to everyone in our Australian Office and the New South Wales government's dedicated unit, who work alongside Rory. Finally, we'd like to say thank you to our Board and Executive team – including Peter, Philip, Helen, Janet, Nicky, Ian, Elizabeth and Zhi, who have all played crucial roles in making BIT what it is today.

What makes BIT such a special place has been our ability to blend academic research with real-world policy interventions. We are especially indebted to some of the finest minds in behavioural science who have supported and mentored the team over the years. Top of this list is Richard Thaler, who helped set up the team in 2010 and has been a trusted advisor and friend ever since. Alongside Richard has been the inspirational Cass Sunstein, who together with Richard wrote the book *Nudge*, and who continues to offer support and guidance to the eponymous unit. We would like to thank our group of UK academic advisors, including Professor Theresa Marteau, Professor Peter John and Professor Nick Chater. They have all been with BIT since its earliest days. And we'd also like to thank the academics at Harvard University, and in particular Professor Max Bazerman, who co-chairs Harvard's Behavioral Insights Group and has been a long-term source of advice and support to the team.

We have further been fortunate enough to have the support of two superb Cabinet secretaries, first Lord Gus O'Donnell and more recently Sir Jeremy Heywood, who have overseen the BIT's core government programmes from 2010. Both Gus and Jeremy continue to be big supporters of our work, and we are indebted to them for their help over the years

In writing this book, we would also like to say a big thank you to Jo Stansall, our editor at Michael O'Mara Books. Jo and the MOM team have been hugely supportive throughout the writing process. We are immensely grateful for their help and suggestions along the way.

What has made this book so interesting and appealing was the blurring of the professional and the personal. At its core, it's about applying the insights we developed at work to our everyday lives. Which brings us to our final and most important thank you, which is to our families, and in particular our ever supportive, insightful and understanding wives – Sophie and Elaine. This book has happily coincided for us both with the wonderful challenges of starting new families, which has made their patience and encouragement for early-morning, late-night and weekend writing even more remarkable. Thank you.

BIBLIOGRAPHY

Ayres, I., *Carrots and Sticks: Unlock the Power of Incentives to Get Things Done;* Bantam Dell Publishing Group (2010)

Bazerman, M. and D. Moore, *Judgment in Managerial Decision Making* (eighth edition); John Wiley & Sons (2013)

Behavioural Insights Team, 'EAST: Four Simple Ways to Apply Behavioural Insights'; Behavioural Insights Team (2014)

Behavioural Insights Team: 'Update Report: 2015–16'; Behavioural Insights Team (2016)

Cialdini, R., *Influence: The Psychology of Persuasion* (revised edition); HarperCollins (1984)

Dolan, P., *Happiness by Design: Change What you Do, Not How you Think;* Penguin (2014)

Duckworth, A., *Grit: The Power of Passion and Perseverance;* Scribner Book Company (2016)

Dunn, E. and M. Norton, *Happy Money: The New Science of Smarter Spending;* Oneworld Publications (2013)

Dweck, C., *Mindset: How You Can Fulfil Your Potential;* Random House (2012)

Gigerenzer, G., *Gut Feelings: The Intelligence of the Unconscious;* Penguin (2007)

Gollwitzer, P. and P. Sheeran, 'Implementation Intentions and Goal Attainment: A Meta Analysis of Effects and Processes' (2002)

Grant, A., *Give and Take: A Revolutionary Approach to Success;* Weidenfeld & Nicolson (2013)

Halpern, D., *Inside the Nudge Unit: How Small Changes Can Make a Big Difference*; WH Allen (2015)

Harford, T., *Adapt: Why Success Always Starts with Failure*; Little, Brown (2011)

Harford, T., *Messy: How to Be Creative and Resilient in a Tidy-Minded World*; Little, Brown (2016)

Haynes, L., O. Service, B. Goldacre and D. Torgerson, 'Test, Learn, Adapt: Developing Public Policy with Randomised Controlled Trials' (2012)

Kahneman, D., *Thinking, Fast and Slow*; Penguin (2011)

Lally, P., 'How Habits are Formed', European Journal of Social Psycology (2010)

Layard, R., *Happiness: Lessons from a New Science*; Penguin Press (2005)

Locke, E. and G. Latham, 'Building a Practically Useful Theory of Goal Setting and Task Motivation: A 35-Year Odyssey'; *American Psycologist* (2002)

Mullainathan, S. and E. Shafir, *Scarcity: Why Having Too Little Means So Much*; Allen Lane (2013)

New Economics Foundation, The, 'Five Ways to Wellbeing' (2008).

Oettingen, G., *Rethinking Positive Thinking: Inside the New Science of Motivation*; Current (2014)

Tetlock, P. and D. Gardner, *Superforecasting: The Art and Science of Prediction*; Random House (2014)

Thaler, R., *Misbehaving: The Making of Behavioural Economics*; Penguin (2015)

Thaler, R. and C. Sunstein, *Nudge: Improving Decisions about Health, Wealth and Happiness*; Penguin (2008)

Soman, D., *The Last Mile: Creating Social and Economic Value from Behavioural Insights*; University of Toronto Press (2015)

Syed, M., *Black Box Thinking: The Surprising Truth about Success*; John Murray (2015)

NOTES

Foreword

1. HMG (2010), 'The Coalition: Our Programme for Government'.
2. For a broader account of the work of the Behavioural Insights Team, see D. Halpern (2015), *Inside the Nudge Unit: How Small Changes Can Make a Big Difference.*
3. Oettingen, G. (2014), *Rethinking Positive Thinking: Inside the New Science of Motivation*; Hofmann, S., A. Asnaani, I. Vonk, A. Sawyer and A. Fang (2012), 'The Efficacy of Cognitive Behavioral Therapy: A Review of Meta-analyses'.

Introduction

1. We have changed the names of the individuals referred to in this book whenever they have been participants in trials. The names of people working at the Behavioural Insights Team have not been changed.
2. Kahneman drew on the work of Keith Stanovich and Richard West in setting out the 'fast' and 'slow' systems. These are also known as 'System 1' (fast) and 'System 2' (slow).
3. Kahneman, D. (2011), *Thinking, Fast and Slow.*
4. Thaler, R. and C. Sunstein (2008), *Nudge: Improving Decisions about Health, Wealth and Happiness.*
5. Ibid.
6. Mullainathan, S. and E. Shafir (2013), *Scarcity: Why Having Too Little Means So Much.*
7. Haynes, L., O. Service, B. Goldacre and D. Torgerson (2012), 'Test, Learn, Adapt: Developing Public Policy with Randomised Controlled Trials'.
8. Bell, C. (2013), 'Inside the Coalition's controversial 'Nudge Unit''; *Daily Telegraph*

Chapter 1: Set

1. Dunn, E., L. Aknin and N. Norton (2009), 'Spending Money on Others Promotes Happiness'.

2. Halpern, D. (2015), *Inside the Nudge Unit: How Small Changes Can Make a Big Difference.*

3. Diener, E. (1984), 'Subjective Well-being'; Layard, R. (2005), *Happiness: Lessons from a New Science*; Seligman, M. (2002), *Authentic Happiness: Using the New Positive Psychology to Realize Your Potential for Lasting Fulfillment*; Gilbert, D. T. (2007), *Stumbling on Happiness.* For an overview of the wider literature, you might also look at Chapter 9 ('Well-Being') of Halpern, D. (2015), *Inside the Nudge Unit: How Small Changes Can Make a Big Difference.*

4. Halpern (2015), *Inside the Nudge Unit.*

5. Dunn, E., D. Gilbert and T. Wilson (2011), 'If Money Doesn't Make You Happy Then You Probably Aren't Spending It Right'; Dolan, P. (2014), *Happiness by Design: Change What you Do, Not How you Think.*

6. We have adapted our five factors from the excellent report produced by the New Economics Foundation, which was commissioned by the UK government to ensure that the wellbeing research could be used by individuals and institutions interested in improving people's wellbeing. The report is called 'Five Ways to Wellbeing'.

7. Dolan, P., T. Peasgood and M. White (2008), 'Do We Really Know What Makes Us Happy? A Review of the Economic Literature on the Factors Associated with Subjective Wellbeing'.

8. Ibid.

9. Halpern (2015), *Inside the Nudge Unit.*

10. Holt-Lunstad, J., T. Smith and J. Layton (2010), *'Social Relationships and Mortality Risk: A Meta-analytic Review'.* Cited in Halpern (2015), *Inside the Nudge Unit.*

11. Dolan, Peasgood and White (2008), 'Do we Really Know What Makes Us Happy?'

12. Layard, R., A. Clark and C. Senik (2012), 'The Causes of Happiness and Misery', Chapter 3 of *World Happiness Report.*

13. Australian Government (2012), 'Benefits to Business: The Evidence for Investing in Worker Health and Wellbeing'.

14. National Health Service (2015): 'Exercise for Depression'.

15. The New Economics Foundation (2008), 'Five Ways to Wellbeing'.

16. Huppert, cited in New Economics Foundation (2008), 'Five Ways to Wellbeing'.

17. Van Bovan, L. and T. Gilovich (2003), 'To Do or to Have? That Is the Question'.

18. New Economics Foundation (2008), 'Five Ways to Wellbeing'.

19. Greenfield, E. and N. Marks (2004), 'Formal Volunteering as a Protective Factor for Older Adults' Psychological Well-being'.

20. *Harvard Business Review*, January–February issue (2012), 'The Science Behind the Smile'. See also Gilbert, D. T. (2007), *Stumbling on Happiness*.

21. The Behavioural Insights Team (2013), 'Applying Behavioural Insights to Charitable Giving'.

22. Soman, D. and M. Zhao (2011), 'The Fewer the Better: The Number of Goals and Savings Behavior'.

23. Ibid.

24. Emmons, R. and L. King (1988), 'Conflict among Personal Strivings: Immediate and Long-term Implications for Psychological and Physical Wellbeing'.

25. Locke, E. and G. Latham (2002), 'Building a Practically Useful Theory of Goal Setting and Task Motivation: A 35-Year Odyssey'.

26. Sheeran, P. (2002), 'Intention–Behavior Relations: A Conceptual and Empirical Review'.

27. Gollwitzer, P. and P. Sheeran (2002), 'Implementation Intentions and Goal Attainment: A Meta Analysis of Effects and Processes'.

28. Inman, J. and L. McAlister (1994), *'Do Coupon Expiration Dates Affect Consumer Behavior?'*.

29. Ariely, D. and K. Wertenbroch (2002): 'Procrastination, Deadlines, and Performance'.

30. Syed, M. (2015), 'Viewpoint: Should We All Be Looking for Marginal Gains?'.

31. Pidd, H. (2016), 'How Scientific Rigour Helped Team GB's Saddle-Sore Cyclists on Their Medal Trail'.

32. Miller, G. (1956), 'The Magical Number Seven, Plus or Minus Two: Some Limits on our Capacity for Processing Information'.

33. Rea, P. (2016), 'How to Go from Zero to Marathon in Six Months'.

34. Bandura, A. and D. Schunk (1981), 'Cultivating Competence, Self-Efficacy, and Intrinsic Interest through Proximal Self-Motivation'.

35. Boice, B. (1990), *Professors as Writers: A Self-Help Guide to Productive Writing.*

36. Highsmith, J. (2004), *Agile Project Management: Creating Innovative Products.* Addison-Wesley Professional.

37. Latham, G. and G. Seijts (1999), 'The Effects of Proximal and Distal Goals on Performance on a Moderately Complex Task'. Cited in Locke and Latham (2002), 'Building a Practically Useful Theory of Goal Setting and Task Motivation'.

38. Baumeister, R. and J. Tierney (2012), *Willpower: Rediscovering the Greatest Human Strength.*

Chapter 2: Plan

1. Fraser, M. and D. Soumitra (2008), 'Barack Obama and the Facebook Election'.

2. Nickerson, D. W. and T. Rogers (2010), 'Do You Have a Voting Plan? Implementation Intentions, Voter Turnout, and Organic Plan Making'.

3. Ibid.

4. Ibid.

5. *Daily Mail* (2015): 'Why well-off women are most likely to have a problem with alcohol: Richest fifth are three times more likely to drink every day than those on lower incomes'.

6. Sutherland, R. (2013), 'If you want to diet, I'm afraid you really do need one weird rule'; *Spectator*

7. Thefastdiet.co.uk (2016), 'How Does the Fast Diet Work?'.

8. Mata, J., P. Todd and S. Lippke (2009), 'When Weight Management Lasts: Lower Perceived Rule Complexity Increases Adherence'.

9. Milkman, K., J. Beshears, J. Choi, D. Laibson and B. Madrian (2011), 'Using Implementation Intentions Prompts to Enhance Influenza Vaccination Rates'.

10. Ibid.

11. Gollwitzer and Sheeran (2002), 'Implementation Intentions and Goal Attainment'; Gollwitzer, P. and V. Brandstatter (1997), 'Implementation Intentions and Effective Goal Pursuit'.

12. Gollwitzer and Sheeran (2002), 'Implementation Intentions and Goal Attainment'.

13. Ibid.; Milkman, Beshears, Choi, Laibson and Madrian (2011), 'Using Implementation Intentions Prompts to Enhance Influenza Vaccination Rates'.

14. Oettingen, G., G. Honig and P. Gollwitzer (2000), 'Effective Self-Regulation of Goal Attainment'.

15. Oettingen (2014), *Rethinking Positive Thinking*.

16. Robins, L., D. Davis and D. Goodwin (1974), 'Drug Use by US Army Enlisted Men in Vietnam: a Follow-Up on their Return Home'.

17. Bernheim, D. and A. Rangel (2004), 'Addiction and Cue-Triggered Decision Processes'; also cited in Dolan (2014), *Happiness by Design*.

18. Bernheim and Rangel (2004), 'Addiction and Cue-Triggered Decision Processes'.

19. Jacobs, L. (2013), *The History of Popcorn!*

20. Neal, D., W. Wood, M. Wu and D. Kurlander (2011), 'The Pull of the Past: When Do Habits Persist Despite Conflict With Motives?'.

21. University of Southern California (2011), 'Habit Makes Bad Food Too Easy to Swallow'.

22. Lally, P. (2010), 'How Habits are Formed'.

23. Lally, P. and B. Gardner, (2011), 'Promoting Habit Formation'.

24. Lally, P. (2010), 'How Habits are Formed'.

25. Neal, Wood, Wu and Kurlander (2011), 'The Pull of the Past'.

26. Lally (2010), 'How Habits are Formed'.

Chapter 3: Commit

1. Dellavigna, S. and U. Malmendie (2006), 'Paying Not to Go to the Gym'.

2. Read, D., G. Loewenstein and S. Kalyanaraman (1999), 'Mixing Virtue and Vice: Combining the Immediacy Effect and the Diversification Heuristic'.

3. Ibid.

4. Ibid.

5. Bryan, G., D. Karlan and S. Nelson (2010), 'Commitment Devices'.

6. Cialdini, R. (1984), *Influence: The Psychology of Persuasion*.

7. Ashraf, N., D. Karlan and W. Yin (2006), 'Tying Odysseus to the Mast: Evidence from a Commitment Savings Product in the Philippines'.

8. Ibid.

9. Huyghe, E., J. Verstraeten, M. Geuens and A. Van Kerckhove (2016): 'Clicks as a Healthy Alternative to Bricks: How Online Grocery Shopping Reduces Vice Purchases'.

10. Asch, S. (1955), 'Opinions and Social Pressure'.

11. Deutsch, M. and H. Gerard (1955), 'A Study of Normative and Informational Social Influence upon Individual Judgment'.

12. Ibid.

13. There was a lovely twist in this experiment, which involved some of the participants writing down their answers on 'Magic Pads' and then immediately erasing the answers. This variant also cut down on the errors (though only by a third), which shows the power of writing something down even if you know that the only person who will ever see it is you.

14. Thomas, A. and R. Garland (1993), 'Supermarket Shopping Lists: Their Effect on Consumer Expenditure'.

15. Moriarty, T. (1975), 'Crime, Commitment and the Responsive Bystander'.

16. Cialdini (1984), *Influence*.

17. Locke and Latham (2002), 'Building a Practically Useful Theory of Goal Setting and Task Motivation'.

18. Kerr, N. and R. MacCoun (1985), 'The Effects of Jury Size and Polling Method on the Process and Product of Jury Deliberation'.

19. Olson, R. (2014), 'What Makes for a Stable Marriage', blog at http://www.randalolson.com/2014/10/10/what-makes-for-a-stable-marriage/

20. Francis, A. and H. Mialon (2014), "A Diamond is Forever' and Other Fairy Tales: The Relationship between Wedding Expenses and Marriage Duration'.

21. Gollwitzer, P., P. Sheeran, V. Michalski and A. Seifert (2009), 'When Intentions Go Public Does Social Reality Widen the Intention–Behavior Gap?'

22. https://www.youtube.com/watch?v=sCX_TcKDr4w

23. Ayres, I. (2010), *Carrots and Sticks: Unlock the Power of Incentives to Get Things Done.*

24. Baumeister, R. and Tierney, T. (2012), *Willpower.*

25. http://www.glowcaps.com/

Chapter 4: Reward

1. Burgess, S., R. Metcalfe, S. Sadoff (2016), 'Understanding the response to financial and non-financial incentives in education: Field experimental evidence using high-stakes assessments'.

2. Giné, X., D. Karlan and J. Zinman (2009), 'Put Your Money Where Your Butt Is: A Commitment Contract for Smoking Cessation'.

3. Ibid.

4. http://qje.oxfordjournals.org/content/115/3/791.short

5. Kahneman, D. and A. Tversky (1992), 'Advances in Prospect Theory: Cumulative Representation of Uncertainty'.

6. Kahneman, D., J. Knetsch and R. Thaler (1991), 'The Endowment Effect, Loss Aversion, and Status Quo Bias'.

7. Loewenstein, G., J. Price and K. Volpp (2014), 'Habit Formation in Children: Evidence from Incentives for Healthy Eating'.

8. Belot, M., J. James and P. Nolen (2014), 'Incentives and Children's Dietary Choices: A Field Experiment in Primary Schools'.

9. Frey, B. and F. Oberholzer-Gee (1997), 'The Cost of Price Incentives: An Empirical Analysis of Motivation Crowding-Out'.

10. Lacetera, N., M. Macis and R. Slonim (2012), 'Will There Be Blood? Incentives and Displacement Effects in Pro-Social Behaviour' and Titmuss, R. (1970), *The Gift Relationship*.

11. Gneezy, U. and Rusticini, A. (2000): A Fine is a Price.

12. Ordóñez, L. D., M. E. Schweitzer, A. D. Galinsky and M. H. Bazerman (2009), 'Goals Gone Wild: The Systematic Side Effects of Overprescribing Goal Setting'; and Ariely, D., U. Gneezy, G. Loewenstein and N. Mazar (2009), 'Large Stakes and Big Mistakes'.

13. Finkelstein, E., H. Hua, U. Gneezy and M. Bilger (2015), 'A Randomized Controlled Trial to Motivate and Sustain Physical Activity Among Taxi Drivers Using Financial Incentives'.

14. Anik, L., L. Aknin, M. Norton, E. Dunn and J. Quoidbach (2013), 'Prosocial Bonuses Increase Employee Satisfaction and Team Performance'.

Chapter 5: Share

1. Christakis, M. and J. Fowler (2008), 'The Collective Dynamics of Smoking in a Large Social Network'.

2. Ibid.

3. Thaler, R. (2015), *Misbehaving*.

4. Gigerenzer, G. (2007), *Gut Feelings: The Intelligence of the Unconscious*.

5. Brooks, D. (2011), *The Social Animal: The Hidden Sources of Love, Character, and Achievement*.

6. Flynn, F. and V. Lake (2008), 'If You Need Help, Just Ask: Underestimating Compliance With Direct Requests for Help'.

7. Ibid.

8. Bohns, V. (2016), '(Mis)Understanding Our Influence over Others: A Review of the Underestimation-of-Compliance Effect'.

9. Ibid.

10. Education Endowment Foundation (2016), 'Texting Parents Evaluation Report and Executive Summary'.

11. Bowman-Perrott, L., H. Davis, K. Vannest, L. Williams, C. Greenwood and R. Parker (2013), *Academic Benefits of Peer Tutoring: A Meta Analytic Review of Single-Case Research*.

12. The Education Endowment Foundation (2016), 'Peer Tutoring: Technical Appendix'.

13. Wing, R. and R. Jeffery (1999), 'Benefits of Recruiting Participants with Friends and Increasing Social Support for Weight Loss and Maintenance'.

14. Irwin, B., J. Scorniaenchi, N. Kerr, J. Eisenmann and D. Feltz (2012), 'Aerobic Exercise Is Promoted when Individual Performance Affects the Group: A Test of the Kohler Motivation Gain Effect'.

15. Rogers, T. and K. Bohling (2015), 'Thinking about Texting Parents? Best Practices for School to Parent Texting'.

16. Metcalfe, T. and R. LaFranco (2013), 'Lego Builds New Billionaires as Toymaker Topples Matel'; article at bloomberg.com.

17. Robertson, D. (2013), 'Building Success: How Thinking 'inside the brick' saved Lego'; article in wired.co.uk.

18. https://ideas.lego.com/howitworks.

19. Robertson, D. (2013), *Brick by Brick: How LEGO Rewrote the Rules of Innovation and Conquered the Global Toy Industry*.

20. Fritolay (2014), 'Meet the Lays Do Us a Flavor Winning Flavor'; www.fritolay.com.

21. Grant, A. (2013), *Give and Take*.

22. Christakis and Fowler (2008), 'The Collective Dynamics of Smoking in a Large Social Network'.

23. Ibid.

24. Jebb, S., A. Ahern, A. Olson, L. Aston, C. Holzapfel, J. Stoll, U. Amann-Gassner, A. Simpson, N. Fuller, S. Pearson, N. Lau, A. Mander, H. Hauner and I. Caterson (2011), 'Primary Care Referral to a Commercial Provider for Weight Loss Treatment Versus Standard Care: A Randomised Controlled Trial'.

25. Kast, F., S. Meier and D. Pomeranz (2012), 'Under-Savers Anonymous: Evidence on Self-Help Groups and Peer Pressure as a Savings Commitment Device'.

26. Galton, F. (1907), 'Vox Populi'.

27. Tetlock, P. and D. Gardner (2014), *Superforecasting: The Art and Science of Prediction*.

28. Glazebrook, K. (2016), 'Would You Hire on the Toss of a Coin?'; Blogpost at behaviouralinsights.co.uk

29. Tetlock and Gardner (2014), *Superforecasting*.

30. Harford, T. (2016), *Messy: The Power of Disorder to Transform Our Lives*.

31. We call this process 'ThinkGroup' – an attempt to overcome the phenomenon which Irving Janis called Groupthink, in which 'concurrence-seeking becomes so dominant in a cohesive in-group that it tends to override realistic appraisal of alternative courses of action'.

Chapter 6: Feedback

1. Annual Report of the Chief Medical Officer: Volume Two, 2011: 'Infections and the Rise of Antimicrobial Resistance'.

2. Hallsworth, M., T. Chadborn, A. Sallis, M. Sanders, D. Berry, F. Greaves, L. Clements and S. Davies (2016), 'Provision of Social Norm Feedback to High Prescribers of Antibiotics in General Practice: A Pragmatic National Randomised Controlled Trial'.

3. Luca, M. (2011), 'Reviews, Reputation, and Revenue: The Case of Yelp.com'.

4. Bandura, A. and D. Cervone, (1983), 'Self-Evaluative and Self-Efficacy Mechanisms Governing the Motivational Effects of Goal Systems'.

5. At least that's what they thought was happening. In a mischievous twist beloved of psychology professors, they had arranged that, not only were everybody's goals the same, but so was the feedback – regardless of actual performance. This would give them a purer way

of seeing the effects of feedback – and to see how important it is to understand how it relates to where you want to get to (i.e. your goal).

6. Kivetz calls this the 'illusion of progress', but we prefer to think about the *feeling* of progress when thinking about how this can apply to your personal goals.

7. Goetz, T. (2011), 'Harnessing the Power of Feedback Loops', www.wired.co.uk

8. Veneziano, D., L. Hayden and J. Ye (2010), 'Effective Deployment of Radar Speed Signs'.

9. http://www.stopspeeders.org/options.htm.

10. The Education Endowment Foundation's research is available online. The Feedback entry is here: https://educationendowmentfoundation. org.uk/evidence/teaching-learning-toolkit/feedback.

11. Kellaway, L. (2015), 'A Blast of Common Sense Frees Staff from Appraisals', *Financial Times*.

12. Mueller, C. and C. Dweck (1998), 'Praise for Intelligence Can Undermine Children's Motivation and Performance'.

13. Ibid.

14. Dweck, C. (2012), *Mindset: How You Can Fulfil Your Potential*.

15. Gerber, A., D. Green and C. Larimer (2008), 'Social Pressure and Voter Turnout: Evidence from a Large-Scale Field Experiment'.

16. Ibid.

17. Ibid.

18. The Behavioural Insights Team (2014), 'EAST: Four Simple Ways to Apply Behavioural Insights'.

19. Ipsos MORI and the Behavioural Insights Team (2015): 'Major survey shows Britons overestimate the bad behaviour of other people'.

20. Galdini, R. (1984), *Influence: The Psychology of Persuasion*.

21. Medvec, V., S. Madey and T. Gilovich (1995): 'When less is more: counterfactual thinking and satisfaction among Olympic medalists'.

Chapter 7: Stick

1. Duckworth, A., T. Kirby, E. Taykayama, H. Berstein and K. A. Ericsson (2011): 'Deliberate Practice Spells Success: Why Grittier Competitors Triumph at the National Spelling Bee' and Ericsson, K. A., R. T. Krampe and C. Tesch-Romer (1993), 'The Role of Deliberate Practice in the Acquisition of Expert Performance'.

2. Ericsson, A. and R. Pool (2016), *Peak: Secrets from the New Science of Expertise.*

3. Syed, M. (2015), *Black Box Thinking: The Surprising Truth about Success.*

4. You can download the excellent Freakonomics podcast from their website, including the episode referred to here: http://freakonomics.com/podcast/the-three-hardest-words-in-the-english-language-a-new-freakonomics-radio-podcast/

5. Haynes, Service, Goldacre and Torgerson (2012), 'Test, Learn, Adapt'.

6. OJJDP News at a Glance (2011), 'Justice Department Discourages the Use of "Scared Straight" Programmes'.

7. Ibid.

8. Grant, A. (2008), 'Employees without a Cause: The Motivational Effects of Prosocial Impact in Public Service'.

9. Di Stefano, G., G. Pisano, F. Gino and B. Staats (2016), 'Making Experience Count: The Role of Reflection in Individual Learning'.

10. Kahneman, D., B. Fredrickson, C. Schreiber and D. Redelmeier (1993), 'When More Pain is Preferred to Less: Adding a Better End'.

11. Kahneman (2011), *Thinking, Fast and Slow.*

12. Kahneman, Fredrickson, Schreiber and Redelmeier (1993), 'When More Pain is Preferred to Less'.

Conclusion

1. Harford (2016), *Messy.*

2. We would discuss the chapter before writing anything down; one of us would then set out a bullet-point summary of the structure and the other would then turn it into a full narrative, after which we started a lengthy editing process.

INDEX